National Park Service
U.S. Department of the Interior

Natural Resource Program Center

Prescribed fire resource kit for grassland parks in the Central Grasslands, U.S.: information resources for prescribed fire planning

Natural Resource Report NPS/HTLN/NRR—2008/027

Prescribed fire resource kit for grassland parks in the Central Grasslands, U.S.

information resources for prescribed fire planning

Natural Resource Report NPS/HTLN/NRR—2008/027

Sherry A. Leis
Missouri State University
National Park Service
901 S. National Ave.
Springfield, Missouri 65897

February 2008

U.S. Department of the Interior
National Park Service
Natural Resource Program Center
Fort Collins, Colorado

The Natural Resource Publication series addresses natural resource topics that are of interest and applicability to a broad readership in the National Park Service and to others in the management of natural resources, including the scientific community, the public, and the NPS conservation and environmental constituencies. Manuscripts are peer-reviewed to ensure that the information is scientifically credible, technically accurate, appropriately written for the intended audience, and is designed and published in a professional manner.

Natural Resource Reports are the designated medium for disseminating high priority, current natural resource management information with managerial application. The series targets a general, diverse audience, and may contain NPS policy considerations or address sensitive issues of management applicability. Examples of the diverse array of reports published in this series include vital signs monitoring plans; monitoring protocols; "how to" resource management papers; proceedings of resource management workshops or conferences; annual reports of resource programs or divisions of the Natural Resource Program Center; resource action plans; fact sheets; and regularly-published newsletters.

Views, statements, findings, conclusions, recommendations and data in this report are solely those of the author(s) and do not necessarily reflect views and policies of the U.S. Department of the Interior, NPS. Mention of trade names or commercial products does not constitute endorsement or recommendation for use by the National Park Service.

Printed copies of reports in these series may be produced in a limited quantity and they are only available as long as the supply lasts. This report is also available from the Natural Resource Publications Management website (http://www.nature.nps.gov/publications/NRPM) on the Internet or by sending a request to the address on the back cover.

Please cite this publication as:

Leis, S. L. 2008. Prescribed fire resource kit for grassland parks in the Central Grasslands, U.S.: information resources for prescribed fire planning. Natural Resource Report NPS/HTLN/NRR—2008/027. National Park Service, Fort Collins, Colorado.

NPS D-72, February 2008

Contents

Figures

Tables

Abstract

This prescribed fire resource kit is intended to provide information that can be used in the prescribed fire planning process for parks in the Central Grasslands region. Summary information on ignition sources, <u>fire history</u>, <u>heterogeneity</u>, <u>exotic plant species</u>, and <u>woody control</u> in the Central Grasslands region of the United States are highlighted as important information needs. Seminal research papers on these topics and an additional set of <u>annotated references</u> and websites have been added for readers to reference. Ultimately, the resources in this document will assist with preparation for writing measurable fire management objectives. A companion document includes copies of seminal papers denoted in the annotated bibliography.

Acknowledgements

I am grateful to C. Wienk, D. C. Cummings, D. Twidwell, J. Kolaks and M. DeBacker for providing helpful comments on the manuscript. Thanks also to K. Hase and A. Smith for feedback on the pilot version of this project. The Midwest Regional Fire Management Program Office of the National Park Service as well as the Missouri State University Biology Department also provided support for this project.

Introduction

This prescribed fire resource kit is intended to provide information that can be used in the prescribed fire planning process in the Central Grasslands region. Summary information on ignition sources, fire history, heterogeneity, exotic plant species, and woody control are highlighted as important information needs. Seminal research papers on these topics and an additional set of annotated references and websites have been added for readers to reference. Ultimately, the resources in this document will assist with augmenting staff fire ecology knowledge and preparation for writing measurable fire management objectives (Figure 1).

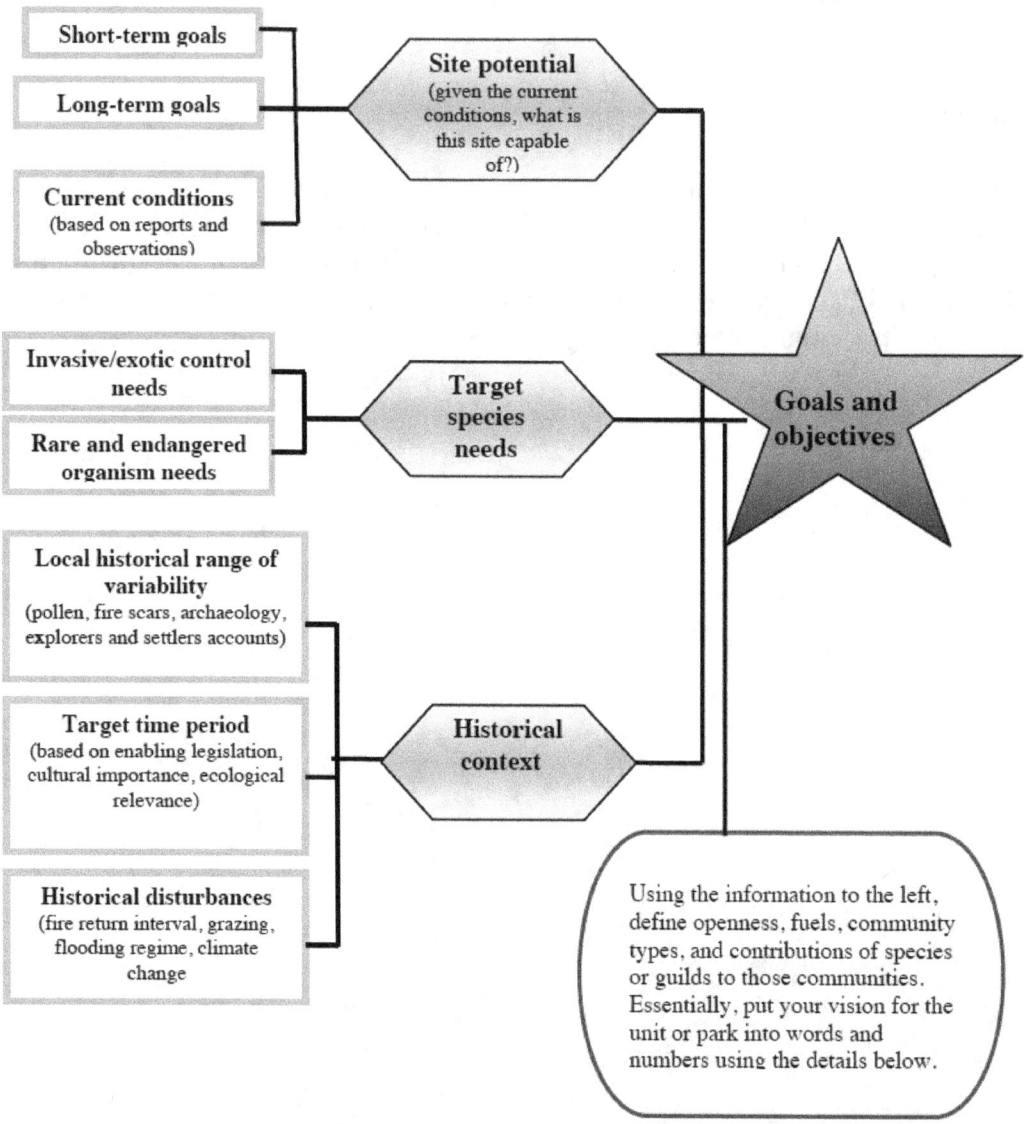

Figure 1. Items for consideration in defining goals and objectives. Historical context most relevant to the park's natural resources, management needs for species of interest, and the potential of each management unit are important elements for understanding the state of the resources and therefore planning for the future.

The National Park Service's Heartland I&M Network and the Midwest Regional Fire Ecology program are excited to assist park staff with the various steps of planning from providing monitoring data to using that data together with research and staff experience to formulate effective and realistic strategies. Development of specific goals and objectives will feed back into the monitoring and fire ecology programs such that monitoring staff will be better able to tailor monitoring and reports to address park management needs. Reader feedback on this document will be used for revisions to make it more useful.

Chapter 1. Summary Reports

1.1 Fire history

Knowledge of historic fire patterns can be instructive in determining an effective schedule for applying fire to the landscape today (Frost 1998). Managers may wish to replicate historical fire patterns or simply use them as a guide when designing new plans. This essay will discuss ignition sources and the components of historical fire return intervals. There are several good review papers (cited herein) which discuss fire history. Anderson (2006) and Bragg (1995) are included in the resource kit as sources of fire history and Guyette et al. 2002 and 2006 are included for information on fire return intervals.

Our historical understanding of fire comes from several sources. Charcoal fragments recovered and dated from soil profiles and sediments, fire scars on trees in an area of interest, written accounts from settlers and Native American histories corroborate physical evidence, and current lightning strikes can be tracked as an analog to the past (Frost 1998). Each of these elements has positive traits, but the weaknesses must be kept in mind. For example, the presence of a fire scar is positive evidence of a fire, but fire can occur without recording a scar (Paulsell 1957). The extent of inference in the data maybe limited by topography, development and other disturbances, as well as climate change. Soil and sediment cores may provide information from a different scale than the one of interest, and written historical accounts may be biased toward reporting of unusual or fantastic events (Earls 2006). Given these biases, it is advisable to consult data from multiple sources whenever possible.

Sediment core and fire scar records show that the composition and distribution of woody plants, particularly trees, in the Great Plains and Central Grasslands regions have fluctuated with changes in climate throughout the historical record (Axelrod 1985; Cook et al. 2004; Nelson et al. 2006; McGuire Bogen and Hotchkiss 2007). Approximately, seven to five million years ago, the climate shifted from cold and wet to warmer and dryer stimulating grassland plants to expand while tree species declined in the Great Plains and Central Grasslands regions (Axelrod 1985). Grasses and trees coexisted during the Pliocene until the ice ages began in the Pleistocene. When the climate trended again toward cool and wet conditions 11000-8000 years ago, pollen records of trees increased until another warm dry trend, 5550 years ago, influenced species distributions and abundances towards the current distribution of grasslands we recognize today. There have also been climatic shifts within the last 2000 years such as the Mediaeval Climatic Anomaly, 900-1250 AD, (warm and dry) and the Little Ice Age, 1250 to 1850 AD, (cool and wet) influencing the expansion and contraction of woodlands (Cook at al. 2004; Nelson et al. 2006; McGuire Bogen and Hotchkiss 2007). Landscapes with greater precipitation and cooler temperatures on the boundaries of the grassland regions continue to fluctuate in dominance between grassland and woodland species especially in the absence of fire and grazing. In much the same way, wooded composition of riparian corridors shrinks and swells with years of drought or ample precipitation. Savannahs and shrublands evidence the fluctuation of woodland to grassland transition zones (Curtis 1959; Anderson and Bowles 1999). These transition zones can be difficult habitats to define spatially and compositionally.

4

Lightning frequency varies regionally in the US (Figure 2). The Southeast, Rocky Mountain, and Great Basin regions receive the greatest number of lightning strikes each year (NOAA 2007). Topography, degree of fuel fragmentation, moisture, and accumulations in these regions lead to proliferation of lightning fires of varying extents. Wildfires ignited by lightning also occur in the tallgrass prairie region, most frequently in July and August. Lightning occurring in the spring, however, is often accompanied by moist fuels and rain limiting a wildfire's extent (Pyne 1984; Bragg 1995). Historically, summer fires had the potential to encompass large areas if conditions were hot and dry. As the landscape became more fragmented with agriculture and urban development, the extent of burned area also decreased.

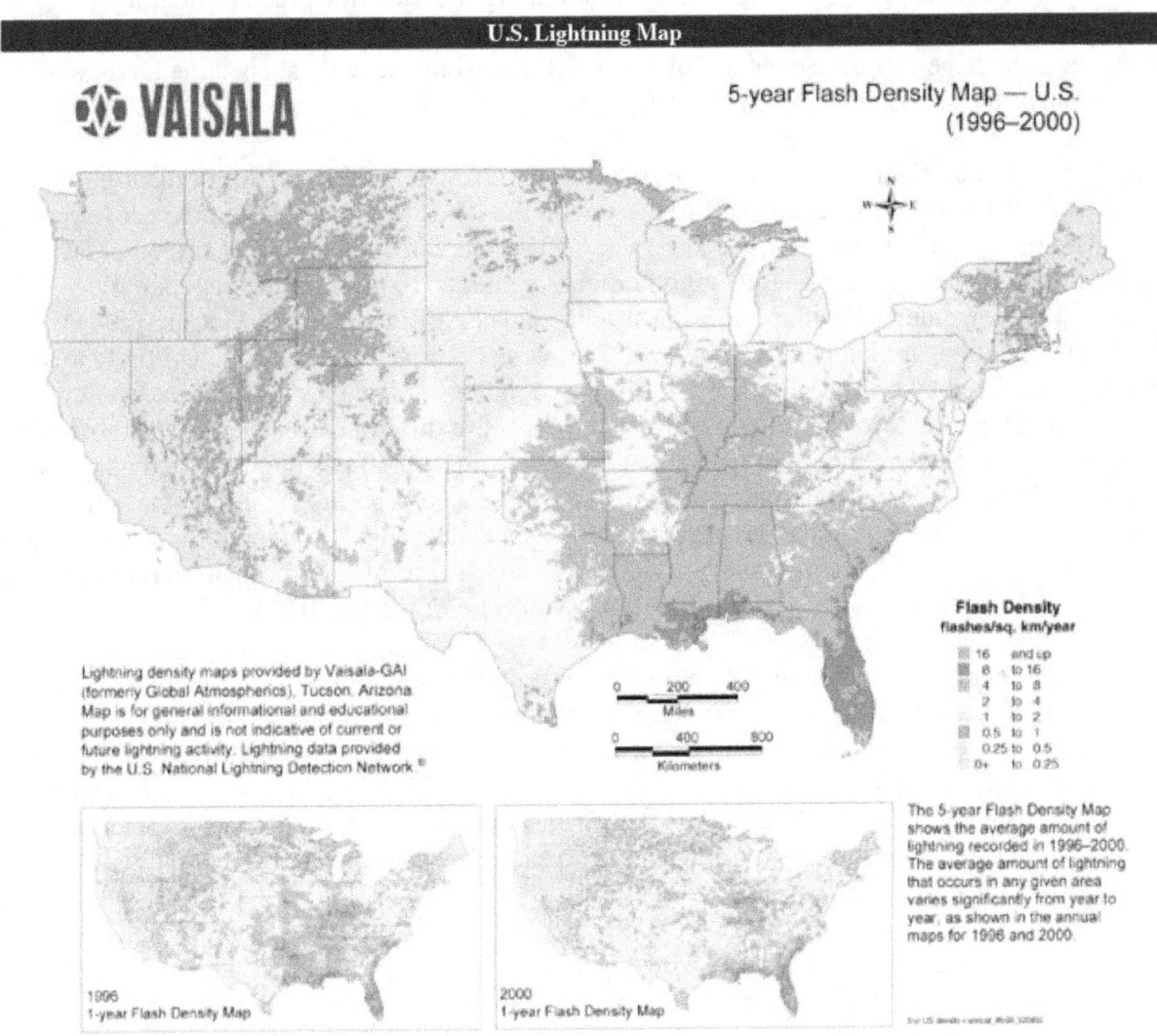

Figure 2. Lightning map for 1996-2000
(http://www.lightningsafety.noaa.gov/lightning_map.htm, Dec. 3, 2007).

Although the role of lightning and anthropogenic ignition sources are discussed briefly below, it is unnecessary to decouple anthropogenic ignition from lightning starts for the present discussion. The extensive history of human use of fire in North America (Bragg 1995; Frost 1998) warrants the inclusive description of historic fire presence for planning purposes rather than decoupling "natural" (lightning) and anthropogenic sources. Great difficulty would be incurred to discern differences in fire effects or calculate accurate fire return intervals if one where to try to attribute effects to one source or another in the tallgrass prairie region. That is not to say that each source doesn't have unique characteristics (Pyne 1984), but that effects on flora and fauna would be difficult to ascertain through background variation.

Historic accounts from settlers provide evidence that fire occurred frequently in the tallgrass prairie region (Curtis 1959; Earls 2006); however, lightning ignition was minimal in the eastern portions (Curtis 1959; Pyne 1984). Anthropogenic ignition was a very important source of both intentional and wildlfires throughout the evolution of the North American tallgrass prairie (Curtis 1959; Pyne 1984; Bragg 1995). Fire was used for a myriad of activities such as hunting, controlling insects, and clearing areas (Curtis 1959; Axelrod 1985; Anderson 2006). Some researchers describe anthropogenic use of fire as a force which actually shaped the landscape rather than as a response to it (Curtis 1959).

Together, lightning fires (occurring in the summer) and Native American fire (occurring in the spring and fall) provide evidence that fire existed on the landscape throughout the year (Howe 1994; Bragg 1995; Sieg 1997; Earls 2006; Pyne 1995). The effect of season of fire on plant composition is muddled because several other factors interact to produce the vegetation measured in field studies (Ewing and Engle 1988; Engle and Bidwell 2001; McCarty 2005). While precipitation and temperature patterns, fire intensity, time since last fire, and fuel moisture can be generalized by season, weather patterns are variable such that a snow and ice event can occur during a period that is normally warm and dry. These differences in weather patterns can influence phenology, an important component of predicting fire effects on plants and animals. The uncertainty created by variability in fire effects by season supports the notion that it is important to continue to provide the process of fire as a disturbance throughout the year as it has occurred historically. Where possible, providing a diverse set of disturbances throughout the year may more closely mimic historical processes and support biodiversity (Howe 1994).

The historic relative contribution of lightning to anthropogenic ignitions varies across North America relative to topography, temperature, precipitation, and human population (Guyette et al. 2006). Rougher terrain equates to heterogeneous fuels and smaller fire compartments resulting in limited fire extents (Frost 1998; Guyette et al. 2002). In a multivariate analysis of fire frequency across the US, Guyette et al. (2006) found that fires occurred more frequently in warmer parts of North America because of longer burn windows, greater fuel accumulations, and human population concentrations.

The influence of human populations on fire return intervals is more complex than previously thought (Guyette et al. 2002). General wisdom was that fire suppression progressed with increased settlement of European immigrants. Guyette et al. (2002) identified a shift in cultural tolerance of fire which was dependant on changes in fuel loads and distribution. The change in acceptability of fire was also correlated unimodally with human population size. Fires tended to increase with population to a threshold density. At that threshold, fuels became fragmented and it became culturally unacceptable for fire to be free on the landscape. Investment in infrastructure and ability to harness fire in confined spaces for energy may have contributed to the cultural shift. McClain and Elzinga (1994) documented a similar phenomenon with historical accounts. They found that settlers in Illinois first began using fire to create safety zones for protection from wildlfire, but later expanded their use of fire to agricultural purposes before finally banning the use of fire without permit.

Table 1. Fire return intervals for grassland parks in the Heartland Network. Data are from Guyette et al. (1982, 1992, 2004, and unpublished data and modeling) unless otherwise noted.

Park	Time period of interest	Population estimation humans/km^2	Mean fire return interval and range of variability (yrs)	Comments
PIPE [a]	Pre-mining	0.03	17.8 (8-25)	
	(1700-1832)	0.30	6.8	
	Intense mining period (1837+)	0.60	2.6 (1-7)	Park focus period
HOME [b]	presettlement	0.03	13.7 (4-24)	
	1860	0.14	9.3 (1-10)	
	1865	0.22	7 (1-10)	
	1870	0.61	1.3 (1-10)	
EFMO [c]	Archaic (5000-1000 BC)	0.06	23.4	EFMO intervals corroborated by sediment cores (McGuire Bogen and Hotchkiss 2007)
	Mound Builders (500 BC-1400 AD)	0.60	3.5 (1-10)	Park focus period
	Late prehistoric (500-1650 AD)	0.24	12.4 (3-20)	
	Historic period (1650-1800 AD)	0.12	19.0 (9-29)	
WICR[d] and GWCA[e]	1700-1800	N/A	5 (2-8)	Dey et al. 2004 predicted MFI for 1710-1830 at 3.7 and 1831-1880 at 7.6.
	1831-1880	N/A	7.6 (6.9-12.5)	
	1870+	N/A	22 (12-32)	
TAPR [f]	*presettlement*	N/A	9 (5-13)	
	1850-1880	N/A	9.3-11.6	Based on Brown and Sieg 1999
	1881+	N/A	2 (1-3)	Earls 2006
HEHO [g]	*Presettlement*	N/A	10 (5-15)	Christiansen, personal communication, Pyne 1984
	1874-1890	N/A	(Rare, >30)	Increased agriculture

[a]Pipestone National Monument, MN [b] Homestead Monument of America, NE [c] Effigy Mounds National Monument, IA, [d] Wilsons Creek National Monument, MO [e] George Washington Carver National Monument, MO, [f] Tallgrass Prairie National Preserve, KS [g] Herbert Hoover National Historic Site, IA

Fire return intervals are generally reported as a range of years or as the mean return interval. The width of the interval depends on several things such as size of the area of interest (scale), topography, and sources for fire data. Large scale maps (Frost 1998, Guyette 2006) sometimes depict less frequent intervals than is currently believed to be appropriate for tallgrass prairie because tree ring data is difficult to acquire on a region-wide basis. Inferences must then be made with lower resolution. Heterogeneous landscapes (e.g., the Ozark mountain region) may also be difficult to summarize since portions of an area may be more fire prone than others. Tree ring data also may underestimate fire occurrence, especially of low intensity fires, so the more frequent side of the fire return interval may often be more accurate. Table 1 describes estimated fire return intervals for prairie parks within the Heartland Network. Several of these intervals were calculated using a model which included local temperature, precipitation, population estimates, and fire scar analysis where available. The models were run for park locations for time periods relevant to each park's mission. Because these data were derived specifically for park localities they represent meaningful estimates.

Understanding of sources of fire and how they interact with the landscape to create the mosaic of habitats within the tallgrass prairie region provides a basis for evaluating fire effects on plants, animals, soils, and water resources. The historical fire return intervals defined both spatially and temporally can serve as a starting place for designing management prescriptions. Current site needs together with specific management goals and objectives will determine appropriate prescribed fire frequency as compared to historic fire return intervals.

Literature Cited

(* included in the resource kit companion)

*Anderson, R. C. 2006. Evolution and origin of the Central Grassland of North America: climate, fire, and mammalian grazers. Journal of the Torrey Botanical Society **133**:626-647.

Anderson, R. C. and M. L. Bowles. 1999. Deep-soil savannas and barrens of the midwestern United States. Pages 155-170 *in* R. C. Anderson, J. S. Fralish, and J. M. Baskin, editors. Savannas, barrens, and rock outcrop plant communities of North America. Cambridge University Press, Great Britain.

*Axelrod, D. I. 1985. Rise of the grassland biome, Central North America. The Botanical Review **51**:163-201.

Bragg, T. B. 1995. The physical environment of Great Plains grasslands. Pages 49-81 *in* A. Joern, and K. H. Keeler, editors. The changing prairie. Oxford University Press, New York.

Brown, P. M. and C. H. Sieg. 1999. Historical variability in fire at the ponderosa pine - Northern Great Plains prairie ecotone, southeastern Black Hills, South Dakota. Ecoscience: **6**:539-574.

Cook, E. R., J. Esper, and R. D. D'Arrigo. 2004. Extra-tropical northern hemisphere land temperature variability over the past 1000 years. Quaternary Science Reviews **23**:2063-2074.

Curtis, J. T. 1959. The vegetation of Wisconsin. The University of Wisconsin Press, Madison, Wisconsin.

Dey, D. C., Guyette, R. P. and M. C. Stambaugh. 2004. Fire history of a forest, savanna, and fen mosaic at White Ranch State Forest. Proceedings of the Upland Oak Ecology Symposium Gen. Tech. Rep. SRS-73. Asheville, NC: U.S. Department of Agriculture, Forest Service, Southern Research Station 132-137..

*Earls, P. 2006. Prairie fire history of the tallgrass prairie National Preserve and the Flint Hills, Kansas. Unpublished manuscript submitted to the National Park Service, Omaha, Nebraska.

Engle, D. M., and T. G. Bidwell. 2001. The response of central North American prairies to seasonal fire. Journal of Range Management. **54**:2-10.

Ewing, A. L., and D. M. Engle. 1988. Effects of late summer fire on tallgrass prairie microclimate and community composition. American.Midland.Naturalist **120**:212-223.

*Frost, C. C. 1998. Presettlement fire frequency regimes of the United States: a first approximation. Pages 70-81 *in* T. L. Pruden , and L. A. Brennan, editors. Fire in Ecosystem Management: Shifting the Paradigm from Suppression to Prescription. Tall Timbers Research Station, Tallahassee, FL.

Guyette, R. and B. Cutter. 1992. Fire history at two sites on the Mark Twain National Forest. A report prepared for the Mark Twain National Forest. Rolla, MO.

Guyette, R. P. and D. C. Dey. 2004. The effects of human abundance on wildland fire, forests, and species abundance. Proceedings of the Upland Oak Ecology Symposium Gen. Tech. Rep. SRS-73. Asheville, NC: U.S. Department of Agriculture, Forest Service, Southern Research Station. 128-131.

*Guyette, R. P., D. C. Dey, M. C. Stambaugh, R. Muzika. 2006. Fire scars reveal variability and dynamics of eastern fire regimes. Pages 20-39 *in* M. B. Dickinson, editor. Fire in eastern oak forests: delivering science to land managers, proceedings of a conference. 2005 November 15-17; Columbus, OH. Gen. Tech. Rep. NRS-P-1. Newtown Square, PA: U.S. Department of Agriculture, Forest Service, Northern Research Station.

Guyette, R. P. and E. A. McGinnes. 1982. Fire history of an Ozark Glade. Transactions of the Missouri Academy of Science **16**:85-93.

*Guyette, R. P., Muzika, R. M., and D. C. Dey. 2002. Dynamics of an anthropogenic fire regime. Ecosystems **5**:472-486.

Howe, H. F. 1994. Managing species diversity in tallgrass prairie: assumptions and implications. Conservation biology **8**:691-704.

9

McCarty, K. 2005. Ecological Management. Pages 37-61 *in* P. Nelson. The terrestrial natural communities of Missouri, , Missouri Natural Areas Committee.

*McClain, W. E. and S. L. Elzinga. 1994. The occurrence of prairie and forest fires in Illinois and other Midwestern states, 1679 to 1854. Erigenia **13**:79-90.

McGuire Bogen, S and S. C. Hotchkiss. 2007. Paleo-environmental investigations of a cultural landscape at Effigy mounds National Monument. National Park Service Great Lakes Northern Forest Cooperative Ecosystem Study Unit. University of Wisconsin, Madison.

Nelson, D. M., F. S. Hu, E. C. Grimm, B. B. Curry, and J. E. Slate. 2006. The influence of aridity and fire on Holocene prairie communities in the Eastern Prairie Peninsula. Ecology **87**:2523-2536.

NOAA. 2007. Lightning map of the United States. http://www.lightningsafety.noaa.gov/lightning_map.htm.

Paulsell, L. K. 1957. Effects of burning on Ozark hardwood timberlands. University of Missouri Agricultural Experiment Station Bulletin No. **640**:1-24. Columbia, MO.

Pyne, S. J. 1984. Introduction to wildland fire: fire management in the United States. Wiley-Interscience, John Wiley & Sons New York.

Pyne, S. J. 1995. World fire: the culture of fire on earth. Henry Holt and company, New York.

Sieg C. H. 1997. The role of fire in managing for biological diversity on native rangelands of the Northern Great Plains. RM-GTR 298, 31-38. US Department of Agriculture, Forest Service.

1.2 The case for <u>heterogeneity</u> in tallgrass prairie

Heterogeneity is defined by Webster's New World Dictionary (2002) as "differing in structure, quality, etc., dissimilar, composed of unlike parts". This generic description of the word transfers well to ecological applications. In grasslands, variation in soils and topography naturally create a degree of heterogeneity resulting in differences in vegetation structure (height and density at ground, mid, and canopy layers), species richness, composition, litter development, and nutrient cycling (Whittaker 1972; Harrison et al. 2003). Historically, grazing animals concentrated feeding on recently burned patches (Vinton et al. 1993; Fuhlendorf and Engle 2001) maintaining a mosaic of areas with different disturbance histories reflected in the plant and soil communities (Glenn et al. 1992). Traditionally, grassland management has sought to overcome inherent variability by managing for homogeneity. For example, clean burns, water distribution, fencing designs, mowing, herbicide usage, fertilizer application, evenly planted restorations, and grazing distributions designed to increase utilization have created homogenous grasslands and habitats to the detriment of some wildlife and plant species.

Heterogeneity may be defined differently at different scales of interest, for example at the 1 m^2 scale heterogeneity may have different implications than at the management unit or park scales (Collins and Smith 2006). Soil type may drive variation at large scales, while management actions may account for variation at more local scales. At the park scale, we can evaluate heterogeneity by comparing management units or patches to learn whether structure and composition vary within or between patches.

Organisms have varied habitat structure requirements (Grant and Birney 1979; Grant et al. 1982; Knopf and Samson 1997; Fuhlendorf et al. 2006). Species need tall dense structure, open sparse habitats, a combination of dense and sparse structures, as well as the intervening possibilities. Grassland birds as a guild require heterogeneous habitat (Winter et al. 2005). Henslow's sparrows, for example, are known to prefer undisturbed habitat with rank growth and dense litter (Herkert 2003) while upland sandpipers prefer areas with a portion of bare ground and less dense vegetation (Dechant et al. 2003). Birds such as quail and prairie chickens require open areas with short dense plants for courtship, mid-range structure for brood rearing, and dense cover for nesting (Bidwell et al. 2003). While prairie chickens don't tolerate trees in their habitat, quail require a certain portion of shrubs or trees for winter cover (Bidwell et al. 2003, 2007). Similar patterns of species habitat preferences for different patch types can be found for insects (Engle et al. 2008) and small mammals (Schramm and Willcutts 1983; Clark et al 1989; Tanner and Kneipp 2007). It is possible to provide habitat needs for a variety of organisms simultaneously within a pasture or landscape by managing for heterogeneity (Fuhlendorf et al. 2006). Providing a variety of areas in different stages of recovery from disturbance may provide greater species richness at the park or landscape scale (Connell 1978).

When possible, it is important to think about heterogeneity and management goals in terms of the presence or absence of habitat types in the surrounding landscape (Knopf and Samson1997). Where grasslands are small and isolated, much more needs to be achieved on a piece of land. In a grassland context where neighbors provide one habitat type, the park or pasture could complement that to complete the range of variability needed for wildlife in the landscape. Whenever possible, the scale and extent of both management and heterogeneity should be defined (Parr and Andersen. 2006). For example, if creating heterogeneity with fire alone, a management goal may be to burn 65% of a 1000-acre patch but to burn only 30% of a 50-acre patch. These goals may result in very different burn prescriptions.

Increased habitat variability also translates into greater heterogeneity in fuel loads across the landscape. Heterogeneous landscapes may also help manage wildfire severity by altering rates of spread and fire-line complexity (Kerby et al. 2006). Patch size affects fuel loads and the resulting fire intensity. A heterogeneous landscape may slow the advance of wildfires making them easier and safer to manage.

There are many ways to infuse heterogeneity into an area. Simply varying disturbance patterns across the park or landscape within and between years will provide more variety in habitats. Pyric herbivory (aka patch burn grazing, focal grazing, or rotational grazing without fences) has been implemented at a number of research sites and private ranches to test the effects of variability in habitat structure within a land management unit. This grazing system draws on the synergy created by the interaction of fire and grazing animals (Fuhlendorf and Engle 2001; Rogers 2007). One portion (often 1/3, but number of patches depends on the site) of a management unit is burned each year and livestock are released (bison and cattle have been tested with this system, but other native ungulates also seem to respond). Grazers move freely between unburned and burned areas so the only fencing required is an exterior one. The recently burned areas are typically the most attractive and receive intense grazing (Fuhlendorf and Engle 2004). When a new patch is burned, the grazers move and recovery begins on the previously burned area. At this point three types of habitat structure are created. The cycle continues until all the patches have been burned and then the rotation repeats.

Although, grazing is an excellent way to achieve this type of structural diversity (Fuhlendorf 2006), it is not an appropriate tool for all land management units. In tallgrass prairie, it is often difficult to provide the element of open ground for wildlife. Development of alternatives to grazing may rely on creativity on the part of managers to achieve a similar effect. While burning alone reduces canopy cover and litter, recovery occurs very quickly perhaps even by mid-season especially where there is ample rainfall. Mowed areas can attract grazers in the absence of fire (Chris Helzer, TNC land manager, personal communication 2006), but to better simulate the selectivity of grazing, mowing could be done in a "messy" fashion so that portions of the patch remain unmowed and/or mowed at varying heights. Shade structures are also a useful tool to relocate grazing animals. Light discing may also be an option in some areas where invasive species establishment is not a concern.

If fire is the only tool available, it is important to consider varying the season of burn as well as frequency of burn (Howe 1994; Sieg 1997). Historically, fire occurred throughout the growing season. Lightning fires were more frequent during the summer months while Native Americans burned from April through October (Bragg 1995). McClain and Elzinga (1994) explain that Native Americans in Illinois used fire almost exclusively during Indian summer in the fall. Spring burning was later instituted by settlers to protect their properties from fall fires. Plant phenology interacts with weather (and other environmental factors), fire intensity, and disturbance history to produce the resulting variation in stress or stimulus to the plant community at any given time. When season of burn is tested, studies both show positive affects on forb diversity (Gibson, 1989; Bragg 1995) and neutral effects (Engle and Bidwell 2001). Some early fire studies demonstrated a clear increase in warm season grasses and subsequent decrease in forbs after spring burns (McMurphy and Anderson 1965; Wright and Bailey 1982; Gibson 1989). Annual spring burning in prairies in the absence of grazing has been shown to maintain low levels of woody cover but at the expense of diversity (Collins 1992). Likewise, long fire return intervals in tallgrass prairie can result in lower species diversity (Collins and Barber 1985).

Altering the types of fire applied may also help to infuse heterogeneity into land management units. Fire plans often call for ring-fire techniques, but there are many other techniques that can be safely employed such as strip head-fire, backing fire, and spot ignition. Using different techniques may shift fire intensities to different parts of the unit stimulating plant production and habitat variability to different parts of the management unit (Bidwell et. al 1990; Morrison 2002).

Concerns about heterogeneity may not be a priority for each park or land unit. The size and landscape context of the park may make discussions of heterogeneity irrelevant. However, where managing for heterogeneity is an option many benefits are possible, for example managing, for heterogeneity can reduce invasive species, increase species richness of plants and wildlife, and reduce infrastructure needs (Cummings et al. 2007).

Literature Cited

(* included in the resource kit companion)

Bidwell, T. G., D. M. Engle, and P. L. Claypool. 1990. Effects of spring headfires and backfires on tallgrass prairie. Journal of Range Management 43:209-212.

Bidwell T., S. Fuhlendorf , S. Harmon, R. Horton, R. Manes,R. Rodgers, S. Sherrod, S. Wolfe. 2003. Ecology and management of the Greater Prairie-Chicken in Oklahoma. Oklahoma State University Extension Circular E-969.

Bidwell, T. G., R. E. Masters, M. Sams. 2007. Oklahoma Bobwhite Quail Habitat Evaluation and Management Guide. Department of Wildlife Conservation. Oklahoma State University, Division of Agricultural Sciences and Natural Resources, Oklahoma Cooperative Extension Service. E-904. version 7.

Bragg, T. B. 1995. The physical environment of Great Plains grasslands. Pages 49-81 in A. Joern, and K. H. Keeler, editors. The changing prairie. Oxford University Press, New York.

Clark, B. K., D. W. Kaufman, E. J. Finck, and G. A. Kaufman. 1989. Small mammals in tall-grass prairie: patterns associated with grazing and burning. Prairie Naturalist 21:177-184.

Collins, S. L. 1992. Fire frequency and community heterogeneity in tallgrass prairie vegetation. Ecology 73:2001-2006.

Collins, S. L., and S. C. Barber. 1985. Effects of disturbance on diversity in mixed-grass prairie. Vegetation 64:87-94.

*Collins, S. L., and M. D. Smith. 2006. Scale-dependent interaction of fire and grazing on community heterogeneity in tallgrass prairie. Ecology **87**:2058-2067.

Connell, J. H. 1978. Diversity in tropical rain forests and coral reefs. Science **199**:1302-1310.

Cummings, D. C., S. D. Fuhlendorf, and D. M. Engle. 2007. Is altering grazing selectivity of invasive forage species with patch burning more effective than herbicide treatments? Rangeland Ecology and Management **60**:253-260.

Dechant, J. A., M. F. Dinkins, D. H. Johnson, L. D. Igl, C. M. Goldade, B. D. Parkin, and B. R. Euliss. 2003. Effects of management practices on grassland birds: Upland Sandpiper. Northern Prairie Wildlife Research Center, Jamestown, ND. Northern Prairie Wildlife Research Center Online. http://www.npwrc.usgs.gov/resource/literatr/grasbird/upsa/upsa.htm (Version 12DEC2003).

Engle, D. M., and T. G. Bidwell. 2001. The response of central North American prairies to seasonal fire. Journal of Range Management. **54**:2-10.

Engle, D. M., S. D. Fuhlendorf, A. Roper, and D. M. Leslie, Jr. 2008. Invertebrate Community Response to a Shifting Mosaic of Habitat. Rangeland Ecology and Management **61**:55-62.

*Fuhlendorf, S. D. and D. M. Engle. 2001. Restoring heterogeneity on rangelands: ecosystem management based on evolutionary grazing patterns. Bioscience **51**:625-632.

Fuhlendorf, S. D. and D. M. Engle. 2004. Application of fire--grazing interaction to restore a shifting mosaic on tallgrass prairie. Journal of Applied Ecology **41**:604-614.

*Fuhlendorf, S. D., W. C. Harrell, and D. M. Engle. 2006. Should heterogeneity be the basis for conservation? Grassland bird response to fire and grazing. Ecological Applications **16**:1706-1716.

Gibson, D. J. 1989. Hulbert's study of factors effecting botanical composition of tallgrass prairie. Proceedings of the eleventh North American prairie conference. Prairie pioneers: ecology, history, and culture. University of Nebraska Printing, Lincoln, Nebraska. 1989:115-133.

Glenn, S. M., S. L. Collins, and D. J. Gibson. 1992. Disturbances in tallgrass prairie: local and regional effects on community heterogeneity. Landscape Ecology **7**:243-251.

Grant, W. E., and E. C. Birney. 1979. Small mammal community structure in North American grasslands. Journal of Mammalogy **60**:23-36.

Grant, W. E., E. C. Birney, N. R. French, and D. M. Swift. 1982. Structure and productivity of grassland small mammal communities related to grazing-induced changes in vegetative cover. Journal of Mammalogy **63**:248-260.

Harrison, S., B. D. Inouye, and H. D. Safford. 2003. Ecological Heterogeneity in the Effects of Grazing and Fire on Grassland Diversity. Conservation biology **17**:837-845.

Herkert, J. R. 2003. Effects of management practices on grassland birds: Henslow's Sparrow. Northern Prairie Wildlife Research Center, Jamestown, ND. Northern Prairie Wildlife Research Center Online. http://www.npwrc.usgs.gov/resource/literatr/grasbird/hesp/hesp.htm (Version 12DEC2003).

Howe, H. F. 1994. Managing species diversity in tallgrass prairie: assumptions and implications. Conservation biology **8**:691-704.

Kerby, J. D., S. D. Fuhlendorf, and D. M. Engle. 2006. Landscape heterogeneity and fire behavior: scale-dependent feedback between fire and grazing process. Landscape Ecology **22**:511-516.

Knopf, F. L., and F. B. Samson. 1997. Conservation of grassland vertebrates. Pages 273-289 *in* F. L. Knopf, and F. B. Samson, editors. Ecology and conservation of Great Plains verebrates. Springer-Verlag, New York.

McMurphy, W.E. and K.L. Anderson 1965. Burning Flint Hills range. Journal of Range Management **18**:265-269.

*McClain, W. E. and S. L. Elzinga. 1994. The occurrence of prairie and forest fires in Illinois and other Midwestern states, 1679 to 1854. Erigenia **13**:79-90.

Morrison, D. A. 2002. Effects of fire intensity on plant species composition of sandstone communities in the Sydney region. Austral Ecology **27**:433-441.

Parr, C. L., and A. N. Andersen. 2006. Patch mosaic burning for biodiversity conservation: a critique of the pyrodiversity paradigm. Conservation biology **20**:1610-1619.

Rogers, R. 2007. New Answers to burning questions. Kansas Wildlife and Parks **April**:2-8.

Schramm, P. and B. J. Willcutts. 1983. Habitat selection of small mammals in burned and unburned tallgrass prairie. Pages 49-55 *in* R Brewer, editor. Eighth North American Prairie Conference. Western Michigan University, Kalamazoo, Michigan, Western Michigan University.

Sieg C. H. 1997. The role of fire in managing for biological diversity on native rangelands of the Northern Great Plains. RM-GTR 298, 31-38. US Department of Agriculture, Forest Service.

Tanner, C. and G. Kneipp. 2007. Effects of prescribed fire on small mammals at Spotsylvania Court House Battlefield. Park Science 24:1-3

Vinton, M. A., D. C. Hartnett, E. J. Finck, J. M. Briggs. 1993. Interactive effects of fire, bison (Bison bison) grazing and plant community composition in tallgrass prairie. American Midland Naturalist **129**:10-18.

15

Websters new world dictionary and thesaurus. 2002. Agnes, M. and C. Laird,editors. 2nd edition. Hungry minds, Inc. New York.

Whittaker, R. H. 1972. Evolution and measurement of species diversity. Taxon **21**:213-251.

Winter, M., D. H. Johnson, and J. A. Shaffer. 2005. Variability in vegetation effects on density and nesting success of grassland birds. Journal of wildlife management **69**:185-197.

Wright, H. A. and A. W. Bailey. 1982. Fire ecology: United States and Southern Canada. John Wiley & Sons, New York.

1.3 Exotic plant species control

The goal of this summary report is to provide a framework for making decisions on exotic plant species control relative to available resources and treatment options. In this summary report, we cannot cover all the possible exotic species you might have at your park, but treatment options for the 20 most dominant exotic species across the Heartland Network (Table 2) are discussed. Native, invasive, woody plants are treated in the following summary paper in this chapter of the toolkit.

Table 2. Top 20 high priority invasive plants of parks in the Heartland Network (ranked by total percent cover, not corrected for park area (courtesy of Craig Young).

Species	Common Name	Rank
Alliaria petiolata	garlic mustard	4
Berberis thunbergii	Japanese barberry	7
Bromus inermis	smooth brome	3
Cirsium arvense	Canada thistle	13
Elaeagnus umbellata	autumn olive	15
Frangula alnus	glossy buckthorn	16
Lespedeza cuneata	sericea	9
Ligustrum vulgare	European privet	5
Lolium spp	fescue	17
Lonicera japonica	Japanese honeysuckle	2
Lonicera morrowii	Morrow's honeysuckle	18
Lysimachia nummularia	creeping jenny	14
Melilotus officinalis	yellow sweet clover	10
Morus alba	white mulberry	19
Phalaris arundinacea	reedcanary grass	6
Poa compressa/pratensis	bluegrass	8
Poa pratensis	Kentucky bluegrass	12
Rhamnus cathartica	common buckthorn	20
Robinia pseudoacacia	Black locust	11
Rosa multiflora	multiflora rose	1

Exotic species concern every land manager globally and critical decisions about how best to use limited resources to control exotics and simultaneously protect native species and biodiversity must be made. For National Park Service Resource Managers, these decisions become part of the planning process for their parks. Documents such as the Resource Stewardship Strategy and Fire Management Plan include descriptions of the priority areas to treat and the type of treatment deemed most appropriate.

When only limited resources, including time and labor, are available managers must make decisions on what plants to control and in which areas. Potential prevention strategies such as cleaning mowing and spraying equipment between treatment areas and surveillance on park and neighboring properties also require additional planning and implementation investments. Spot treatment of small newly detected infestations often requires fewer resources than treatment of widespread populations. Developing strategies for invasive species often involves trade-offs.

There are four basic strategies for allocating resources to invasive species treatment (Smith 2008).

1. *Tackle the most widespread invasives that are affecting native plant communities.* This option offers the most emphasis on protecting natural communities but disturbed areas will have to be addressed as sources of reinfestation. However, widespread invasives are often beyond our ability to eradicate or control. This option may be the least efficient use of time and money.

2. *Work to eradicate those species that are just becoming established but have a history of invading native plant communities in other states or areas.* This option has the advantage of addressing the problem early while there is hope for containing the spread saving time and money in the long-run. Sometimes implementation is difficult because the species isn't yet perceived to be a problem. There is the chance that the species will not be as aggressive in your area because of different climate, soils, and/or land use than in other areas currently infested.

3. *Protect the best examples of natural communities from all invasive species, accepting that the species will become widespread on other, untreated sites.* This option will require continued treatment at boundaries as species will reinvade from the surrounding landscape, but will preserve examples of functioning native ecosystems for study and biodiversity protection. Limiting treatment focus to good quality communities will minimize the number of acres for which treatment is required.

4. *Control those species that are most likely to compromise your ability to reach your management objectives on each tract.* This option is a practical way to allocate resources based on individual area goals. On a site with rare species, control of invasives will target those exotics that harm the rare species. There is a risk in that we often don't know the effects of invasives on particular native species.

(More information on choosing control strategies can be found at http://www.cabi-bioscience.ch/wwwgisp/100Toolkitfin.pdf). Once a strategy is chosen, goals and objectives for exotic species as a group or for individual species can be designed. These goals and objectives should include amounts, locations, and time period to be achieved. Developing goals and objectives will require knowledge of species, monitoring data, field observations, and control methods. Monitoring data and reports can be obtained from the Heartland Network directly or at http://science.nature.nps.gov/im/units/htln/innp.cfm.

Treatment options by species
The following list of treatment recommendations was produced as a reference guide for control of exotic plants in the parks within the HTLN network. Links to key internet resources and books are imbedded within summaries for each species and are annotated at the end of the review.

Treatment recommendations are based around fire as a management tool. Fire shaped bullets preceding species names indicate fire as a potential control technique. Specific descriptions for herbicide application can be found in the sources cited. Control effectiveness can often be enhanced by applying multiple stressors in a coordinated effort such as burning to stimulate germination or reduce standing dead biomass and following up with an herbicide. The burn can enhance the efficacy of the herbicide application in this manner (Masters and Sheley 2001). Herbicide treatment effectiveness can sometimes vary by region and soil type because the chemicals react differently to soil chemistry and plant phenology. It is important to consider that removing plants can create bare ground which may be susceptible to reinvasion. Methods that encourage native species while simultaneously eradicating invasive species may circumvent the creation of bare ground. Herbicide suggestions are not an endorsement of any particular manufacturer. Please follow manufacturer specifications when applying products.

Alliaria petiolata (garlic mustard)

Timing: Treat with fire or herbicide early before other plants begin to green up (April) or in the fall. It is best if temperatures are above 40° F

Control: For small infestations, cut the stems low to the ground. Pulling also works but be careful not to disturb the soil as it can stimulate seed germination. Remove plants from the site in garbage bags and landfill. For larger populations, herbicide with 0.5-..75% glyphosate with surfactant (http://www.dowagro.com/ivm/invasive/invasive.htm). Repeated fall or spring burns can also eliminate it *if* burns are intense and thorough. Where burns are not complete, follow up with herbicides in unburned areas or non-burn years. http://mdc.mo.gov/nathis/exotic/vegman/eleven.htm

Berberis thunbergii Japanese barberry

Timing: Unspecified, plants green up early in the spring for easy identification.

Control: Prescribed fire has controlled this species. Cutting, pulling, and digging early in the spring are also effective as is triclopyr in a cut stump application (Czarapata 2005, http://www.dnr.state.wi.us/invasives/fact/barberry.htm)

Bromus inermis (smooth brome)

Mobility of smooth brome depends on temperature and precipitation. Cooler moister climates seem to struggle more with control than warm dry climates. Where smooth brome is less invasive, it can provide good grassland bird habitat if managed properly.

Timing: Burn when tillers elongate (boot stage), usually early May.

Control: If native tallgrass species make up > 20% of the plant community and tillers have elongated (have at least 5 leaves) but have not developed an inflorescence, burning can be effective. Otherwise, consider herbicide application and possibly reseeding. Mowing will prevent seed set. http://www.npwrc.usgs.gov/resource/plants/sbrome/burn.htm. One study (unpublished) found herbicide with imazapic following an April prescribed fire (plants were 10-15 cm tall) to be more effective than burning alone (Hendrickson and Jund 2005, http://www.ars.usda.gov/research/publications/publications.htm?SEQ_NO_115=17308 7).

○   *Cirsium arvense* (Canada thistle)

Timing: Burn in late spring (May-June). Avoid early spring because it can stimulate reproduction. Root reserves are lowest prior to flowering (Stumpf et al. 1994).

Control: Burn annually for the first three years. An initial increase in the population may occur followed by a decrease (http://www.npwrc.usgs.gov/resource/plants/exoticab/efficirs.htm). Burning may be most effective when root reserves are lowest prior to or immediately post flowering. Translocation of chemicals to rhizomes will be more effective as plants are rebuilding root reserves post flowering increasing efficacy of treatments. Cutting and pulling can be effective on smaller populations if treated persistently. Descriptions of chemical and biological control can be found in the link above. Glyphosate, 2-4-D, and Aminopyralid can be used on large populations, see manufacturer specifications.

•   *Elaeagnus umbellate* (autumn olive)

Timing: Unspecified

Control: Prescribed fire listed as ineffective, see herbicide recommendations at http://www.inhs.uiuc.edu/chf/outreach/VMG/autolive.html. Czarapta (2005) recommends cutting and herbicide treatment with metsulfuron-methyl with surfactant. Miller (2003) also has detailed instructions for treatment.

○   *Frangula alnus* (glossy buckthorn)

Timing: Burn in early spring and fall, apply cutting treatments in dormant season

Control: Prescribed fire annually or biannually until seedbank is exhausted (2-3 years). Cutting to improve fuel development may be required. Small plants can be pulled or dug; larger plants must be girdled or cut followed by stump treatment. Cutting and herbicide treatments can be done in the dormant season. See http://dnr.wi.gov/invasives/fact/buckthorn_gloss.htm for details.

○   *Lespedeza cuneata* (sericea)

Timing: Burn late June – July, herbicide timing varies with active ingredient used

Control: Spring fire should be avoided unless followed up with herbicide in the same growing season. Spring fire stimulates germination and can help to exhaust the seed bank if a secondary treatment is used. Summer fire has not yet been shown to conclusively decrease sericea. Research is pending. A number of herbicides can be used; some herbicides should be used during different stages of the vegetative cycle. Direct foliar spray; 2% Garlon 4 + surfactant (Remedy Ultra ®, Pasturegard®, and Escort® are also feasible. Apply Remedy Ultra® and Pasuregard® June-July, Escort® in August or early September). Mowing 1 to three months prior to herbicide application may assist in control. Mowing in the bud stage will reduce root reserves. Herbicides are most effective on 3-year old plants. Seedlings don't have enough leaf area to absorb adequate amounts of herbicide (personal communication W. Fick, Kansas State University). More herbicide details at http://www.dowagro.com/PublishedLiterature/dh_003c/0901b8038003cad3.pdf?filepath=ivm/pdfs/noreg/010-50165.pdf&fromPage=GetDoc

- *Ligustrum vulgare* (European privet)

Timing: Mechanical and chemical treatments in August-December

Control: Fire not listed as effective. Herbicide and cutting treatments recommended by Miller (2003) and Czarapata (2005). Miller offers detailed herbicide recommendations.

Lolium spp formerly *Festuca* and recently changed to *Schedonorus spp.* (fescue)

Timing: Burn in April/May, prior to emergence of warm season grasses, or late fall after killing frosts and a subsequent warm up period.

Control: Prescribed fire in the spring or fall alone, may retard growth. For heavier infestations use prescribed fire then the following year herbicide in the late fall after killing frosts and a warm up that will stimulate growth. Follow up with a spring fire.

Lonicera japonica (Japanese honeysuckle)

Timing: Burn in spring

Control: Cut or burn vines or burn 1-2 years prior to herbicide treatment. Follow conventional recommendations with triclopyr or glyphosate with surfactant. Crossbow® has also been found to be effective. More herbicide recommendations at: http://www.dowagro.com/PublishedLiterature/dh_003a/0901b8038003a6f3.pdf?filepath=ivm/pdfs/noreg/010-50223.pdf&fromPage=GetDoc

Lonicera morrowii (Morrow's honeysuckle)

Timing: Burn in spring

Control: Prescribed fire can kill seedlings and topkill mature plants making stump treatments more feasible. Treatments should be repeated until infestation is under control. Pulling young plants is feasible, but avoid soil disturbance. A variety of herbicides are recommended in Czarapata (2005), field personnel in Missouri have used a basal bark treatment of Remedy Ultra® (triclopyr) with Stalker® (imazapyr) after fall leaf drop. Use care with imazapyr in sensitive areas as it may leach in the soil. See http://dnr.wi.gov/invasives/fact/honeysuckle_morrow.htm for additional suggestions on chemical and mechanical control.

Lysimachia nummularia (creeping jenny/moneywort)

Timing: Burn or spray in early spring or late fall when other plants are dormant

Control: Controlled burns can be effective (Czarapata 2005). Pulling and herbicide may also be effective. Seeding with native plants can also reduce populations.

Melilotus officinalis

Timing: Burn in April/May

Control: Hand pulling is effective for small populations. Prescribed fire in April of year 1 and in May of year 2. Sequence is repeated two years later.

- *Morus alba*

Timing: Unspecified

Control: Fire not listed as an effective control. Herbicides triclopyr or imazapyr may be effective (Czarapata 2005).

Phalaris arundinacea (reedcanary grass)

Timing: Burn in late spring

Control: http://www.ipaw.org/invaders/reed_canary_grass/draft_rcg_table_sm.pdf provides a matrix of treatment options for a variety of situations. In short, fire can be used in conjunction with another treatment such as herbicide. Burning in late spring to remove litter and standing dead biomass may improve herbicide effectiveness. If the infestation is mature, mowing treatments may be needed to prepare the stand for burning. This species responds to increased light so do not burn in the early spring (before the natives begin growth) or in late fall without a secondary treatment or you'll just make it mad. In cases of heavy infestation, planting to an intermediate crop such as corn, can prepare the area for restoration.

Poa compressa/pratensis (bluegrass/Kentucky bluegrass)

Timing: Burn in spring, before native species green up and when *Poa* flowers are still sheathed. Fall burning may be less effective. If burning in the fall, try burning after a killing frost and subsequent warm up as for fescue

Control: Burn in a rotation to encourage native species competition, but annual spring burning for 3 or more years may be needed to gain control (Stumpf et al. 1994). Herbicides can also be used on degraded sites see (Czarapta 2005) or http://www.npwrc.usgs.gov/resource/plants/exoticab/effipoap.htm. Mowing is not an effective treatment, but early spring grazing in a warm season prairie may give native species a competitive edge (Stumpf et al. 1994).

Rhamnus spp. (buckthorn species)

Timing: Burn in late April or late May (when root reserves are low).

Control: Prescribed fire will kill seedlings and shrubs if adequate fuel is present. Continue burning annually or biannually for 5-6 years to eradicate this group of species. For herbicide and cutting treatments see: http://www.inhs.uiuc.edu/chf/outreach/VMG/buckthorn.html

- *Robinia pseudoacacia* (black locust)

Timing: Unspecified.

Control: Fire is minimally effective. Cutting and herbicide treatments will be most effective, see: http://www.inhs.uiuc.edu/chf/outreach/VMG/blocust.html

Rosa multiflora (multiflora rose)

Timing: July (mowing), unspecified (fire).

Control: Fire can be used to keep this plant under control and hamper establishment. For eradication of small populations pulling, grubbing, or removing individual plants may be effective only if all roots are removed. More extensive populations should be mowed or cut 3-6 times each season for 2-4 years or herbicided, see: http://www.inhs.uiuc.edu/chf/outreach/VMG/mrose.html or http://mdc.mo.gov/nathis/exotic/vegman/seventee.htm.

Web resources

http://dnr.wi.gov/invasives/pubs/manuallist.htm#EXOTIC
Provides details for controlling a host of exotic species. May draw from Czarapata 2005 for information.

http://www.ipaw.org/invaders/reed_canary_grass/draft_rcg_table_sm.pdf
An excellent resource for reedcanary grass control.

http://www.inhs.uiuc.edu/chf/outreach/VMG/VMG.html
An excellent manual for treating several exotic species.

http://invasivespecies.nbii.gov/models.html
General principles for invasive control including biological control. Links to the Illinois Natural History Survey management guide for species specific control.

http://www.invasivespecies.net/
Extensive searchable database. Includes plant biology as well as control recommendations.

http://mdc.mo.gov/nathis/exotic/vegman/
Manual for controlling a host of exotic species in Missouri.

http://www.npwrc.usgs.gov/resource/plants/sbrome/burn.htm
Describes a research project and model for controlling smooth brome.

http://www.npwrc.usgs.gov/resource/plants/exoticab/effipoap.htm.
Description of treatments for Poa pratensis.

http://www.npwrc.usgs.gov/resource/plants/exoticab/efficirs.htm
Description of treatments for Cirsium arvense.

http://tncweeds.ucdavis.edu/handbook.html
Weed Control Methods Handbook:Tools and Techniques for Use in Natural Areas. Gives specific instructions for various herbicides and techniques.

http://www.cabi-bioscience.ch/wwwgisp/100Toolkitfin.pdf
A comprehensive manual for invasive species. For help on prioritizing control efforts page down to page 122.

http://www.vmanswers.com/labels.aspx?pid=33
BASF herbicide application labels and recommendations.

http://www.dowagro.com/range/ and http://www.dowagro.com/ivm/invasive/
Dow AgroSciences herbicide application labels and recommendations for range plants and invasive plants respectively.

http://www.dupont.com/cgi-bin/ag/prodsearch/start.cgi
Dupont herbicide application labels and recommendations.

Literature Cited

(* included in the resource kit companion)

Czarapata, E. J. 2005. Invasive plants of the Upper Midwest: an illustrated guide to their identification and control. University of Wisconsin Press.

Hendrickson, J. R., Lund, C. B. 2005. Control of smooth brome and Kentucky bluegrass using fire and fire plus chemical in the northern Great Plains. Abstract. Presented at the Invasive Species Workshop on April 5-7, 2005, Bismarck, ND.

*Masters, R. E., and R. L. Sheley. 2001. Principles and practices for managing rangeland invasive plants. Journal of Range Management. **54**:502-517.

Miller, J. H. 2003. Nonnative invasive plants of the Southern forests: a field guide for identification and control. Revised. Gen. Tech. Rep. SRS-62. Asheville, NC: U.S. Department of Agriculture, Forest Service, Southern Research Station.

Smith, T. 2008. Strategies for treating invasive species. Missouri Natural Resources Conference: Get Ready for Change: Ensuring Resource Sustainability in an iPod® World. Lake of the Ozarks, Missouri. January 30-February 1, 2008.

Stumpf, J. A., J.Stubbendieck, and C. H. Butterfield. 1994. An assessment of exotic plants at Scotts Bluff National Monument and Effigy Mounds National Monument. Final Report to Midwest Regional Office of the National Park Service.

1.4 Woody Control

This essay will review ecology of woody species in the Central Grasslands region by examining biology and control measures for a suite of common plants. Historically, fire and grazing/browsing disturbances influenced by soils and climatic conditions acted to determine the abundance of woody plants in North America (see chapter 1.1; Axelrod 1985). Woody species can be both beneficial and unwanted depending on the amount, species, and context, hence monitoring plays a critical role in maintaining the integrity of grasslands vis-à-vis woody plant encroachment. Consistent mechanisms are yet to be determined that relate fire effects on woody plants to fuels, weather, and fire behavior, but generalizations are available that are of use in constructing management plans.

First, I must define to which species "woody" refers. The Heartland Network monitoring staff assign species to one of 11 guilds (Table 3). Species are grouped into guilds based on similar features of growth habit, leaf characteristics, stem structures, root structures, and reproduction traits (Kindscher and Wells 1995). Native and exotic trees and shrubs are included in the woody plant guild. Tree species found in grasslands such as persimmon (*Diospyros virginiana*), eastern redcedar (*Juniperus virginiana*), honey locust (*Gleditsia triacanthos*), hackberry (Celtis spp.), and bur oak (*Quercus macrocarpa*) often are intuitive to classify, but common shrubs include New Jersey Tea (*Ceanothus* spp.), buck brush/coral berry (*Symphoricapos* spp.), sumac (*Rhus* spp.), and blackberry/dewberry (*Rubus* spp.). Roses (*Rosa* spp.) are also classified with woody plants, but lead plant (*Amorpha canescens*) is classified as a legume rather than a woody plant. Ability to resprout or reproduce vegetatively is also used as a classification characteristic in some fire ecology literature (Whelen 1995). Inquiries about the guild classification of specific species can be directed to HTLN staff or the USDA plants website also provides a wealth of information about North American plants (http://plants.usda.gov) including growth habit.

Table 3. HTLN guild categories used to classify plants.

Guild Name
annual and biennial forbs
cool-season grasses
ephemeral spring forbs
ferns
grass-like forbs
legumes
spring forbs
succulents
summer/fall forbs
warm-season grasses
woody species

Grassland managers purposefully monitor woody populations with the knowledge that woodlands encourage an entirely different suite of plants and animals, have different mechanisms for nutrient cycling, soil retention, and water usage (Risser et al. 1981; Maestas et al. 2003; Chapman et al. 2004; Hornecastle et al. 2005; Bresherars 2006). From a landscape perspective, soil type and precipitation are the primary abiotic factors associated with woody plant invasion potential (Wright and Bailey1982). The combination of precipitation and soils produce a potential range of possible ecosystems. Historical and observed communities are further determined by ecological disturbances. Current trends in land use (e.g., increased agriculture and exurban development), ecosystem fragmentation, and elevated atmospheric carbon dioxide levels favor the expansion of woody species (Bragg and Hulbert 1976; Archer et al. 1995; Briggs et al. 2002b) whereas, fire and grazing/browsing interact to limit the distribution and abundance of a variety of woody species (Curtis 1959; Anderson and Bowles 1999). Biotic factors that negatively affect woody species (fire and browsing) can moderate the landscape scale effects of climate change which favor the progression to shrublands and woodlands. For example, current climatic patterns promote the expansion of eastern redcedar, but the use of fire can deter transition to cedar thickets in the Central Grasslands region (Owensby et al. 1973). However, threshold conditions exist whereby ecosystem feedbacks may not be able to overcome the influence of climate change, (e.g., if drought conditions transition a sand prairie into a virtual desert, fire and browsing will not be useful tools; (Brown et al. 1997; Knapp et al. 2008).

Numerous factors are associated with fire effects on woody plants but the degree to which these factors interact to influence fire effects remains unclear within the scientific literature. It is therefore critical to distinguish direct effects from indirect effects in order to identify consistent patterns of fire effects from previous research. Direct effects are defined herein to be those influenced by fire behavior whereas indirect effects are divided into two categories:available resources and status of the meristems. Importantly, fire effects on woody plants differ between resprouting and non-resprouting species. Fire intensity directly influences non-resprouting and resprouting species but a high level of fire-induced mortality has only been observed in non-resprouting species (Briggs et al. 2002a); fire has not been shown to be a successful tool in killing resprouting species (Trollope and Tainton 1986), although it may prevent or slow invasion. Resprouting species are often top-killed with fire but the recovery period and resulting resprouts may be influenced by fire intensity (Whelan 1995).

Fire intensity is an often misunderstood factor influencing fire effects. Fire intensity is measured as heat per unit time per length of the fire front e.g., kJ/s/m (Byram 1959). Fuel loads, fuel moisture, fire residence time, wind speed, relative humidity, and slope all contribute to fire intensity. Fuel load and arrangement contribute to scorch height and completeness of injury to the circumference of the plant's stem. Heterogeneous fuel loads also will likely produce more variable effects on the plant community than homogenous fuels. Of the factors affecting fire intensity, fuel load is the most often recognized. The importance of residence time as a component of fire intensity is under investigation and may help to better predict plant level effects (Twidwell personal communication 2008)

Fire intensity, fire frequency, ignition type (headfire vs backfire), fire type (ground, surface, or crown, soil), and fire history directly influence how much damage may be inflicted to a woody plant (Bond and van Wilgen 1996; Whelan 1995). Of these fire intensity is the most important. The literature is unclear in defining species responses to high or low intensity fires that deliver the same amount of heat. Younger trees tend to be damaged at lower intensities than older ones and thus are more vulnerable to fire (Hare 1965; Wright et al. 1976). Ignition type can influence woody plant stress because head fires move more quickly and produce greater intensity than backfires (Bidwell et al. 1990; Trollope 1978). Mortality on trees encountering headfires can be greater than with other ignition types.

Primary physiological attributes indirectly determining woody plant recovery post-fire are resource availability and status of the meristems (Bond and van Wigen 1996; Richburg et al. 2001). Physical characteristics of woody plants such as hydration level, carbohydrate reserves, bark characteristics, and bud structure also determine susceptibility to injury and ability to recover (Bond and van Wilgen 1996; Whelan 1995). Plant phenology and therefore season are directly related to a plant's vulnerability because the status of hydration and carbohydrate root reserves depend on physiological events like leaf out, flowering, and dormancy (Richburg et al. 2001). Injury from fire occurs by the denaturing of proteins and other chemicals, destruction of cell walls, and disruption of photosynthesis or nutrient and water transport. Some injuries directly cause death, but others can lead to susceptibility to infection by fungus or insects , and loss of carbohydrate reserves can slow recovery or indirectly lead to death (Loescher 1990; Richburg et al. 2001). Positive responses to fire include resprouting, flowering, seed production, and seed germination (Whelan 1995)

Grassland management plans often address woody plant removal, but certainly some woody species provide resources to grassland wildlife such as food, escape and thermal cover, and serve as anchors for islands of biodiversity (Hekert 2003; Hull 2003; Bell 2005; Sudkamp Wells and Fuhlendorf 2005). Although some grasslands naturally maintain low levels of native woody plants because of soil types, moisture and nutrient availability, topography, aspect, and disturbance history, other grasslands, transition zones for example, may experience a great deal of variability in woody cover over time. An alternative planning process to simply eradicating woody plants would include the calculation of thresholds for woody plant abundance at a particular location. For example, certain exotic species may have 0% tolerance. Likewise, Chapman et al. (2004) demonstrated that when eastern redcedar reached 25% total cover, abundance of grassland birds declined to nearly zero. Based on that study an acceptable threshold for eastern redcedar might be set at <9% cover.

For each species below (Table 4), plant biology and ecology is briefly considered followed by information on control measures. A detailed account of many of the species can be found at http://www.fs.fed.us/database/feis/plants/shrub/index.html or http://www.na.fs.fed.us/pubs/silvics_manual/volume_2/silvics_v2.pdf. Herbicide suggestions are not an endorsement of any particular manufacturer. Please follow manufacturer specifications.

Table 4. Woody taxa biology, ecology, and control recommendations specifically addressed in this summary.

Common Name	Scientific Name
Blackberry/dewberry	*Rubus spp.*
Buckbrush/coralberry	*Symphoricarpos spp*
Dogwood	*Cornus spp*
Eastern redcedar	*Juniperous virginiana*
Hardwoods	
Rose	*Rosa spp.*
Sumac	*Rhus spp.*

Rubus spp. (Blackberry/dewberry)

Biology/ecology

Many *Rubus* species have canes that are biennial, but their roots and rhizomes are perennial (DiTomaso 2002; Duncan 1935). Tips of canes that touch the ground may also develop roots. The clonal nature of these plants can lead to formation of large thickets in disturbed areas. Second year canes produce flowers and thus have different patterns of carbohydrate production and transportation than first year canes. First year canes transport carbohydrates from roots primarily in the spring or early summer when shoots are elongating whereas second year canes focus transport of sugars later in the season when they are producing fruits (DiTomaso 2002). Fruits of these plants provide nutrition and thickets provide cover. Monitor populations to evaluate acceptable population thresholds.

Control

Burning and mowing reduce canopy cover in the short-term, but plants are likely to produce additional shoots from the root crown or rhizomes (Johnston and Woodard 1985; Reich et al. 1990). Herbicides may be the most effective choice for control of extensive thickets, however little research has been done to test the effect of timing burns to carbohydrate cycles. Time all treatments to periods when carbohydrate transportation is maximized as discussed in the biology section above (DiTomaso 2002). See http://www.ipm.ucdavis.edu/PDF/PESTNOTES/pnwildblackberries.pdf or http://edis.ifas.ufl.edu/WG006 for specific herbicide recommendations.

Symphoricarpos spp. (Buckbrush/coralberry)

Biology/ecology

Symphoricarpos spp. is clonal via rhizomes and stoloniferous plants have been reported (Duncan 1935). The various species can reproduce by seed, but often reproduce vegetatively (http://plants.usda.gov/, Hauser 2007; McWilliams 2000). The plants of this genus prefer areas with open sunlight in grasslands, canopy gaps in woodlands, and riparian areas. *Symphoricarpos* spp. are also palatable to grazing/browsing animals as well as to birds (Stubbendieck et al. 1997; Tyrl et al. 2002). They also provide escape and thermal cover for wildlife (Tyrl 2002).

Control

Experiments measuring *Symphoricarpos* response to grazing and fire have had varied results (Hauser 2007). Burning can sometimes increase stem density, but it has been shown to decrease density as well. Aldous (1934) found that burning during the plants low point in carbohydrate root reserves (April 10-May 12 in Kansas) led to declines in percent cover, whereas burns at other times in the spring or fall resulted in increased stem density. Much like treating sumac (below), timing treatments to take advantage of vulnerable points in the plant's phenology may lead to the greatest success. Fuel may be limiting in a large colony so a combination of mowing and burning may be needed to build up enough fuel to carry fire through the patch.

Cornus spp. (Dogwoods)

Biology/ecology

Cornus florida is found primarliy in woodland understories, but may extend into transition zones (McLemore 1990). Other species of *Cornus* can be found in grasslands, old fields, wetlands, and along riparian areas. *C. florida* has had high mortality from anthracnose in the eastern part of its range (Jenkins and White 2006). Leaves of *C. florida*. have high calcium content important for nutrient cycling, and all species provide important food sources for birds (Kurz 2004; Jenkins and White 2006). *Cornus* spp reproduce by both seed and vegetative mechanisms. *C. drummondii* has a deeper root system and is more drought tolerant than the other more shallowly rooted species of *Cornus* (McLemore 1990). Dogwoods can be an important winter source of food for birds, so evaluate monitoring data carefully to determine whether populations need control.

Control
Dormant season burns appear to have little effect on reducing *Cornus* spp. (Bowles et al. 1996; Kuddes-Fischer and Arthur 2002; Middleton 2002). A 15-year study at Konza biological station using spring fires revealed that *C. drummondii* was kept in check by an annual fire frequency. Intermediate fire frequency (every four years) increased densities over both low frequency (ever 20 years) and annual burning. Grazing by bison accelerated growth, however (Briggs et al. 2002b). By contrast, two consecutive spring fires in a Kansas gallery forest significantly decreased shrub species including *C. drummundii* (Abrams 1988). Management of *Cornus* spp. with fire may be most effective if planned around plant phenology as described for other species in this summary. Single burns in most cases may not be enough to control this species. If resprouts occur after a fire, plan fires for successive years until management goals are reached. Also, consider using multiple disturbances such as applying a fire and following up with mowing or wicking of herbicides on foliage.

Juniperus virginiana (Eastern redcedar)
Biology
Juniperous virginiana is widely distributed in North America having scale-like leaves and blue seed cones which look like berries (Tyrl et al. 2002). Historical distribution of (*J. virginiana*) was likely confined to shallow soils and rocky outcrops by fire and to a lesser extent, grazing (Tyrl et al. 2002; Ownsby et al. 1973). *J. virginiana*has a shallow fibrous rooting structure allowing it to exploit areas of shallow soil such as glades, but making it vulnerable to tipping in high wind events Trees reach reproductive maturity within 6-7 years and pollen causes severe allergenic responses in many people (Midoro-Horiuti et al. 2001). As *J. virginiana* dominates a grassland, soil carbon is converted to above ground biomass (Norrris et al. 2001) and species diversity may decline (Hornecastle et al. 2004, 2005; Briggs et al. 2005). For more detail on the plant's biology see http://www.fs.fed.us/database/feis/plants/tree/junvir/all.html.

Control
If left unchecked, *J. virginiana* can exapand and proliferate into a cedar forest in 20-40 years (Engle and Kulbeth 1992, Briggs et al. 2002a). *J. virginiana* will not resprout when cut below the lowest limb so cutting is a good technique for fence-lines and large trees. Fire is very effective on small trees less than five feet tall (Engle et al. 1988). Trees over six feet tall may require >4000 lbs of fuel and extreme conditions such as drought for fire to kill them (Buehring et al. 1971, Ortmann et al.1998). Herbicides have been used to kill *J. virginiana* (Anderson 2003), however, this is probably not the most economical control method (Buehring et al. 1971; Ortmann et al.1998; Bidwell and Weir 2007). Grazing plans should consider stocking livestock so that adequate fuel is retained for prescribed fires, otherwise *J. virginiana* may increase without additional mechanical control.

Hardwoods e.g., *Carya* (hickory), *Acer* (maple), *Quercus* (oak) and others

Biology/ecology
Many hardwood species have a prominent taproot which provides stability (red maple is an exception; Brown and Smith 2000). As with the shrub species described herein, many of the hardwood trees present in the woodland grassland interface have means of vegetative reproduction. Although, hickory, oak, and elm species, for example, are likely to resprout from root crowns and/or stumps following disturbance (Brown and Smith 2000), the probability of stump sprouting decreases with tree age (Weigel and Johnson 1998). Carbohydrate reserve storage is important to tree productivity. Carbohydrates are used to support metabolic needs prior to initiation of photosynthesis. Trees that flower prior to leaf out depend on stores longer than those that flower after leaf out. During leaf out, carbohydrate stores shift from roots to buds and stems. Root reserves generally are lowest immediately post flowering then gradually recover, peaking again at the point of leaf drop (Loescher et al. 1990). Seedlings and saplings growing in low light conditions often have smaller root systems and lesser root reserves leaving them more susceptible to disturbance (Brose et al. 2006). Species specific descriptions can be found at http://www.na.fs.fed.us/pubs/silvics_manual/volume_2/silvics_v2.pdf.

Control
Stand demographics and light intensity to the ground are important factors influencing the effect of fire on trees and should be assessed when developing a control strategy. Young trees and seedlings grown in low light conditions are more susceptible to fire than those in open grown, high light conditions; hence a single fire may be more likely to achieve management goals in some situations (Brose et al. 2006). Fire can often top kill younger trees and sprouts subsequently stimulating production of vegetative shoots. Forest research suggests that severe fires that raise soil temperatures adequately can sterilize underground meristems in addition to damaging above ground biomass, in effect killing the plants (Brown and Smith 2000). Oak seedlings, however, have deeper tap roots than other more shallowly rooted species and may instead, benefit from the extreme heat. Conducting fires producing extreme amounts of heat may not always be advantageous to the rest of the community, however. Alternatively, burning over a few consecutive years can reduce saplings and seedlings whereas a single fire or one fire every few years may stimulate reproduction (Brose et al. 2006).

Little research has been done on timing fire to take advantage of phenological deficits in carbohydrate reserves of trees. Timing fires to the post flowering period of target species may provide better control. Likewise, pairing mowing of sprouts with fire may improve control. For example, burning post flowering and then following up with mowing of sprouts prior to leaf drop should leave energy stores depleted for the dormant season. Additional treatment the following year may provide adequate control. Combining cutting treatments with subsequent well-timed burns may also increase treatment efficacy by improving the fuel base.

Herbicide control can be applied using several methods such as cut-stump treatments, hack and squirt, and basal bark treatments. Species differ in their susceptibility to herbicide so knowledge of individual species is required. Hickory stumps sprouts were effectively killed with Garlon 3A® (Walter et al. 2004), but red maple does not respond well to herbicide treatments, for example (Walters and Yawney 1990).

Rosa spp. (Rose)

Biology/ecology

Rosa setigera and *R. multiflora* have vertical roots and reproduce by seed or by rooting at the tips of branches. *Rosa* species have prominent lateral roots which can extend almost a meter or more from the plant and extend downward 10-39 cm from the surface with some tap roots extending more than one meter deep (Duncan 1935; Munger 2002). It is important to positively recognize *R. multiflora* from the native rose species. Stipules at the base of each petiole of *R. multifora* are fringed rather than winged in the native species (Figure 3).

A.   B.

Figure 3. *Rosa multiflora* (A) has fringed comb-line stipules unlike native species (B) (A, http://www.ppws.vt.edu/scott/weed_id/rosmu.htm B, www.illinoiswildflowers.info/prairie/plantx/p...).

Control

Rosa spp. are top killed by fire but resprout vegetatively or regenerate by seed. Control measures for *R. multiflora* are detailed in chapter 1.3 on invasive species. Native rose plants provide important food and cover for wildlife (Munger 2002) so careful consideration of the need for control of native species is warranted.

Rhus spp. (Sumac)

Biology/ecology

Winged sumac (*Rhus copallina*) has lateral roots (rhizomatous) with vertical roots extending at each node. Roots vary in length depending on soil type but have been measured at 16.6 m long and 15-35 cm deep on average. Older plants are in the center of a clump with younger stems growing in a circular pattern around the parent stem. The rate of colony expansion was found to be slower on shallow dry sites, 5.4 m/ over 9 years compared to 7.5 m over 9 years on rich soil (Duncan 1935). Anderson et al. (1970) found that smooth sumac (*Rhus glabra*) was more abundant on limestone breaks than uplands or clay pan soils in the Flint Hills. Biology of winged and smooth sumac appears to be similar although phenology may be slightly different. These species can provide important food sources (berries and bark) to animals like deer, rabbits, and birds and provides song perches for some grassland birds. Ground shading in large colonies reduces flora species richness, but provides thermal cover for livestock and wildlife. Acceptable thresholds for *Rhus* species cover should be established because although sumac is native and an important component of native grasslands, it sometimes increases dominance in communities overtime (Collins and Adams 1983).

Control

Control of *Rhus* species especially sumac, is dependant on timing with carbohydrate reserve fluctuations which are lowest immediately following flowering. Hence, winter and early spring mowing or burning efforts result in an increase in stem density rather than a reduction (Aldous 1934; Adams et al. 1982). Given the clonal nature of sumac, treatments will be most effective if entire clones are treated at once. Shrubs were tracked in a Flint Hills, KS study using annually burned (burned at 3 spring dates), grazed pastures over 10 years. *R. glabra* and *Amorpha canescens* both increased during the study but remained less than 1% cover each. Total shrub cover was greatest in the early spring burned pasture, averaging 1.2%. *R. glabra* increased most in the late spring burn pastures (Anderson et al. 1970). Fire effects on poison ivy (*Toxicodendron radicans)* point to a similar pattern as other *Rhus* species in that control should be timed right after flowering, but be aware that the poison ivy smoke can cause an allergic reaction in the lungs if inhaled (Adams et al. 1982; Pavek 1992; Catling et al. 2002; Tyrl et al. 2002).

Mowing was shown to be most effective when carbohydrate reserves were low, principally right after flowering (early June in Missouri, later in more northern climates (Aldous 1934). Applying a single mowing any other time of the year may increase stem density. Recommendations call for mowing post-flowering and again in the fall to reduce winter storage of carbohydrates. Following this procedure for 2-3 years is recommended (Evans 1983, http://www.inhs.uiuc.edu/chf/outreach/VMG/smsumac.html). Burns should either be applied immediately post-flowering or in combination with mowing. For example, burning in August followed by mowing to cut sprouts prior to leaf drop may be effective (http://www.inhs.uiuc.edu/chf/outreach/VMG/smsumac.html).

Chemical control can also be effective. Glyphosate, picloram, 2, 4-D, and triclopyr have been used (Evans 1983). Herbicides should be applied foliarly during periods of translocation of sugars to and from the leaves, such as during leaf-out in late May-early June or possibly during preparation for dormancy in the fall. Wicking with Tordon 22K® and glyphosate have been found to be effective, observationally (Tunnell et al. 2006a; personal communication Steve Clubine, Missouri Department of Conservation). Wicking may be a better option than spraying in areas of widespread colonization and sensitive native species (Tunnell et al. 2006a). Burning did not increase efficacy of herbicides in a Nebraska study (Tunnell et al. 2006b)

Web resources cited

http://www.fs.fed.us/database/feis/plants/shrub/index.html
Species accounts including fire ecology

http://www.na.fs.fed.us/pubs/silvics_manual/volume_2/silvics_v2.pdf
Description of hardwoods by species

http://www.inhs.uiuc.edu/chf/outreach/VMG/smsumac.html
Sumac control guide

http://www.ipm.ucdavis.edu/PDF/PESTNOTES/pnwildblackberries.pdf

http://plants.usda.gov
Taxonomic database includes distributions, pictures, and links

Literature Cited
(* included in the resource kit companion)

Abrams, M. D. 1988. Effects of prescribed fire on woody vegetation in a gallery forest understory in Northeastern Kansas. Transactions of the Kansas Academy of Science **91**:63-70.

Adams, D. E.; R. C. Anderson; and S.L. Collins. 1982. Differential response of woody and herbaceous species to summer and winter burning in an Oklahoma grassland. *The Southwestern Naturalist*. **27**: 55-61

Aldous, A. E. 1934. Effect of burning on Kansas bluestem pastures. Kansas technical bulletin **38**:3-64.

Anderson, K. L., E. F. Smith, and C. E. Owensby. 1970. Burning bluestem range. Journal of Range Management **23**:81-92.

Anderson, M. D. 2003. Juniperus virginiana. *In* U.S. Department of Agriculture, Forest Service, Rocky Mountain Research Station Fire Sciences Laboratory, producer. Fire Effects Information System, [Online]. Available: http://www.fs.fed.us/database/feis/[2008, January 7].

Anderson, R. C. and M. L. Bowles. 1999. Deep-soil savannas and barrens of the midwestern United States. Pages 155-170 *in* R. C. Anderson, J. S. Fralish, and J. M. Baskin, editors. Savannas, barrens, and rock outcrop plant communities of North America. Cambridge University Press, Great Britain.

Archer, S., D. Schimel, and E. H. Holland. 1995. Mechanisms of shrubland expansion: land use, climate or CO2. Climate Change **29**:91-99.

*Axelrod, D. I. 1985. Rise of the grassland biome, Central North America. The Botanical Review **51**:163-201.

Bell, L. A. 2005. Habitat use and growth and development of juvenile lesser prairie chickens in southeast New Mexico MS, Oklahoma State University.

Bidwell, T. G., D. M. Engle, and P. L. Claypool. 1990. Effects of spring headfires and backfires on tallgrass prairie. Journal of range management **43**: 209-212.

Bidwell, T. G. and J. R. Weir. 2007. Eastern redcedar control and management – best management practices to restore Oklahoma's ecosystems. Oklahoma Cooperative Extension Service NREM-2876.

Bond, W. J. and B. W. van Wilgen. 1996. Fire and Plants. Population and community biology series 14, Chapman and Hall, London.

Bowles, M, J. McBride, N. Stoynoff, and K. Johnson. 1996. Temporal changes in vegetation composition and structure in a fire-managed prairie fen. Natural Areas Journal. **16**: 275-288.

Bragg, T. B., and L. C. Hulbert. 1976. Woody plant invasion of unburned Kansas bluestem prairie. Journal of Range Management **29**:19-24.

Breshears, D. D. 2006. The grassland-forest continuum: trends in ecosystem properties for woody plant mosaics? Frontiers in ecology and the environment **4**:96-104.

Briggs, J. M., G. A. Hoch, and L. C. Johnson. 2002a. Assessing the rate, mechanisms and consequences of conversion of tallgrass prairie to Juniperus virginiana forest. Ecosystems **5**:578-586.

Briggs, J. M., A. K. Knapp, J. M. Blair, J. L. Heisler, G. A. Hoch, M. S. Lett, and J. K. McCarron. 2005. An ecosystem in transition: causes and consequences of the conversion of mesic grassland to shrubland. BioScience **55**: 243–254.

*Briggs, J. M., A. K. Knapp, and B. L. Brock. 2002b. Expansion of woody plants in tallgrass prairie: a fifteen-year study of fire and fire-grazing interactions. American Midland Naturalist **147**:287-294.

Brose, P. H. T. M. Schuler, and J. S. Ward. 2006. Responses of oak and other hardwood regeneration to prescribed fire: what we know as of 2005. Pages 123-135 *in* M. B. Dickinson, editor. Fire in eastern oak forests: delivering science to land managers, proceedings of a conference; 2005 November 15-17; Columbus, OH. Gen. Tech. Rep. NRS-P-1. Newtown Square, PA: U.S. Department of Agriculture, Forest Service, Northern Research Station. http://nrs.fs.fed.us/pubs/8405

Brown, J. K. and J. K. Smith (editors). 2000. Wildland fire in ecosystems: effects of fire on flora. Gen.Tech. Rep. RMRS-GTR-42-vol. 2. Ogden, UT: U.S. Department of Agriculture, Forest Service, Rocky Mountain Research Station.

Brown, J. H., T. J. Valone, and C. G. Curtin. 1997. Reorganization of an arid ecosystem in response to recent climate change. Proceedings of the National Academy of Sciences of the USA 94: 9729–9733.

Buehring, N., P. W. Santelmann, and. M. Elwell. 1971. Responses of eastern red cedar to control procedures. Journal of Range Management **24**:378-382.

Byram, G. M. 1959. Combusion of forest fuels. Pages: 61-89 *in*: K. P. Davis, editor. Forest fire: control and use. McGraw Hill, New York.

Catling, P. M., A. Sinclair, and D. Cuddy. 2002. Plant community composition and relationships of disturbed and undisturbed alvar woodland. Canadian Field-Naturalist **116**:571-579.

Chapman, R. N., D. M. Engle, R. E. Masters, and D. M. Leslie Jr. 2004. Tree invasion constrains the influence of herbaceous structure in grassland bird habitats. Ecoscience **11**:55-63.

Collins, S. L., and D. E. Adams. 1983. Succession in grasslands: Thirty-two years of change in a central Oklahoma tallgrass prairie. Vegetatio **51**:181-190.

Curtis, J. T. 1959. The vegetation of Wisconsin. The University of Wisconsin Press, Madison, Wisconsin.

DiTomaso, J. M. 2002. Wild blackberries. Pest notes publication 7434. University of California, Agriculture and Natural Resources, IPM Education and Publications, UC Statewide IPM Program, University of California, Davis, CA 95616-8620.

Duncan, W. H. 1935. Root systems of woody plants of old fields of Indiana. Ecology **16**:554-566.

Engle, D. M. and J. D. Kulbeth. 1992. The growth dynamics of crowns of eastern redcedar at 3 locations in Oklahoma. Journal of Range Management **45**:301-305.

Engle, D. M. J. F. Stritzke, and P. L. Claypool. 1988. Effects of paraquat plus prescribed burning on eastern redcedar (*Juniperus virginiana*). Weed Technology **2**:171-174.

Evans, J. E. 1983. Literature review of management practices for smooth sumac (*Rhus glabra*), poison ivy (*Rhus radicans*) and other sumac species. Natural Areas Journal **3**:16-26.

Hare, R. C. 1965. Contribution of bark to fire resistance of southern trees. Journal of forestry **63**:248-251.

Hauser, A. S. 2007. Symphoricarpos occidentalis. *In* U.S. Department of Agriculture, Forest Service, Rocky Mountain Research Station, Fire Sciences Laboratory, producer. Fire Effects Information System, [Online]. Available: http://www.fs.fed.us/database/feis/ [2008, January 4].

Herkert, J. R. 2003. Effects of management practices on grassland birds: Henslow's Sparrow. Northern Prairie Wildlife Research Center, Jamestown, ND. Northern Prairie Wildlife Research Center Online. http://www.npwrc.usgs.gov/resource/literatr/grasbird/hesp/hesp.htm (Version 12DEC2003).

Horncastle, V. J., E. C. Hellgren, P. M. Mayer, A. C. Ganguli, D. M. Engle, and D. M. Leslie Jr. 2004. Differential Consumption of Eastern Red Cedar (Juniperus virginiana) by Avian and Mammalian Guilds: Implications for Tree Invasion. The American Midland Naturalist **152**:255–267

Horncastle, V. J., E. C. Hellgren, P. M. Mayer, A. C. Ganguli, D. M. Engle, and D. M. Leslie Jr. 2005. Implications of invasion by Juniperous virginiana on small mammals in the Southern Great Plains. Journal of Mammalogy **86**: 1144–1155.

Hull, S. D. 2003. Effects of management practices on grassland birds: Eastern Meadowlark. Northern Prairie Wildlife Research Center, Jamestown, ND. Northern Prairie Wildlife Research Center Online. http://www.npwrc.usgs.gov/resource/literatr/grasbird/eame/eame.htm (Version 12DEC2003).

Johnston, M. and P. Woodard. 1985. The effect of fire severity level on postfire recovery of hazel and raspberry in east-central Alberta. Canadian Journal of Botany **63**:672-677.

Jenkins, M. A. and P. S. White. 2002. *Cornus Florida* L. mortality and understory composition changes in Western Great Smokey Mountains National Park. Journal of the Torrey Botanical Society **129**:194-206.

Kindscher, K., and P. V. Wells. 1995. Prairie plant guilds: a multivariate analysis of prairie species based on ecological and morphological traits. Vegetatio **117**:29-50.

Knapp, A. K., J. M. Briggs, S. L. Collins, S.R. Archer, M. S. Bret-Harte, B. E. Ewers, D. P. Peters, D. R. Young, G. R. Shaver, E. Pendall, M. B. Cleary. 2008. Shrub encroachment in North American grasslands: shifts in growth form dominance rapidly alters control of ecosystem carbon inputs. Global Change Biology 14:615–623.

Kuddes-Fischer, L. M. and M. A. Arthur. 2002. Response of Understory Vegetation and Tree Regeneration to a Single Prescribed Fire in Oak-Pine Forests. Natural Areas Journal **22**:43-52.

Kurz, D. 2004. Shrubs and woody vines of Missouri. 2nd edition. Missouri Department of Conservation, Jefferson City, Missouri.

Loescher, W. H., T. McCamant, and J. D. Keller. 1990. Carbohydrate reserves, translocation, and storage in woody plant roots. HortScience **25**:274-281.

*Maestas, J. D., R. L. Knight, and W. C. Gilgert. 2003. Biodiversity across a rural land use-gradient. Conservation biology **17**:1425-1434.

McLemore, B. F. 1990. Cornus florida L.—Flowering dogwood. Pages 278–283 *in* R. M. Burns and B. H. Honkala, editors. Silvics of North America. Volume 2. Hardwoods. Agriculture Handbook 654. USDA Forest Service, Washington, D.C., USA.

McWilliams, Jack. 2000. Symphoricarpos albus. *In* U.S. Department of Agriculture, Forest Service, Rocky Mountain Research Station, Fire Sciences Laboratory, producer. Fire Effects Information System, [Online]. Available: http://www.fs.fed.us/database/feis/ [2008, January 4].

Middleton, B. 2002. Winter burning and the reduction of *Cornus sericea* in sedge meadows in Southern Wisconsin. Restoration ecology **10**: 732-730

Midoro-Horiuti, T. R. M. Goldblum, E. G. Brooks. 2001. Identification of mutations in the genes for the pollen allergens of eastern red cedar (*Juniperus virginiana*) Clinical & Experimental Allergy **31**:771–778.

Munger, G. T. 2002. Rosa multiflora. *In* U.S. Department of Agriculture, Forest Service, Rocky Mountain Research Station, Fire Sciences Laboratory, producer. Fire Effects Information System, [Online]. Available: http://www.fs.fed.us/database/feis/ [2008, January 4].

Norris, M. D., J. M. Blair, L. C. Johnson, and R. B. McKane. 2001. Assessing changes in biomass, productivity, and C and N stores following Juniperus virginiana forest expansion into tallgrass prairie. Canadian Journal of Forest Research **31**:1940-1946.

Ortmann, J., J. Stubbendieck, R.A. Masters, G. H. Pfeiffer, and T. B. Bragg. 1998. Efficacy and costs of controlling eastern redcedar. Journal of Range Management **51**:158-163.

Owensby, C. E., K. R. Blan, B. J. Eaton, and O. G. Russ. 1973. Evaluation of eastern redcedar infestations in the Northern Kansas Flint Hills. Journal of Range Management **26**:256-286.

Pavek, D. S. 1992. Toxicodendron radicans. *In* U.S. Department of Agriculture, Forest Service, Rocky Mountain Research Station, Fire Sciences Laboratory, producer. Fire Effects Information System, [Online]. Available: http://www.fs.fed.us/database/feis/ [2008, January 7].

Reich; P. B., M. D. Abrams; D. S. Ellsworth; E. L. Kruger; T. J. Tabone. 1990. Fire affects ecophysiology and community dynamics of Central Wisconsin oak forest regeneration. *Ecology* **71**:2179-2190.

*Richburg, J. A., A. C. Dibble, and W. A. Patterson, III. 2001. Woody invasive species and their role in altering fire regimes of the Northeast and Mid-Atlantic states. Pages 104–111 *in* K. E. M. Galley and T. P. Wilson, editors. Proceedings of the Invasive Species Workshop: the Role of Fire in the Control and Spread of Invasive Species. Fire Conference 2000: the First National Congress on Fire Ecology, Prevention, and Management. Miscellaneous Publication No. 11, Tall Timbers Research Station, Tallahassee, FL.

Risser, P. G., E. C. Birney, H. D. Blocker, S. W. May, W.J . Parton, J. A. Wiens. 1981. The true prairie ecosystem. Hutchinson Ross Publishing Company, Pennsylvania.

Suedkamp Wells, K. M. and S. D. Fuhlendorf. 2005. Comparison of Microclimate at Grassland Bird Nests with Different Substrates. The Prairie Naturalist **37**:21-28.

Stubbendieck, J. S. L. Hatch, and C. H. Butterfield. 1997. North American range plants. 5th edition. University of Nebraska Press, Lincoln.

Trollope, W. S. W. 1978. Fire--a rangeland tool in Southern Africa. Pages 245-247 *in* D. N. Hyder, editor. Proceedings of the first international rangeland congress. Society for Range Management, Denver, Colorado.

Trollope, W. S. W. and N. M. Tainton. 1986. Effect of fire intensity on the grassland bush components of the Eastern Cape Thornveld. Journal of the Grassland Society of South Africa **2**:27-42.

Tunnell, S. J., J. Stubbendieck, and S. Palazzolo. 2006a. Forb response to herbicides in a degraded tallgrass prairie. Natural Areas Journal **26**:72-77.

*Tunnell, S. J., J. Stubbendieck, S. Palazzolo, and R. A. Masters. 2006b. Reducing smooth sumac dominance in native tallgrass prairie. Great Plains Research **16**:45-49.

Tyrl, R. J., R. G. Bidwell, R. E. Masters. 2002. Field guide to Oklahoma plants. Oklahoma State University, Stillwater, Oklahoma.

Walter, W. D. H. E. Garrett and L. D. Godsey. 2004. Response of eastern black walnut to herbicide stump treatment. D. A. Yaussy, A. Hix, D. M. Long, R. P. Goebel, P. Charles, editors. Proceedings 14th Central Hardwood Forest Conference; 2004 March 16 19; Wooster, OH. Gen. Tech. Rep. NE-316. Newtown Square, PA: U.S. Department of Agriculture, Forest Service, Northeastern Research Station: Pp. 52-55.

Walters, R. S. and H. W. Yawney. 1990. Acer rubrum, red maple. *In* R. M. Burns and B. H. Honkala, editors. Silvics of North America: Vol 2, Hardwoods.. Agriculture Handbook 654. U.S. Department of Agriculture, Forest Service, Washington, DC.

Weigel, D. R. and P. S. Johnson. 1998. Stump sprouting probabilities for Southern Indiana oaks. Technical brief TB-NC-7. USDA Forest Service, North Central Research Station.

Whelan, R. J. 1995. The ecology of fire. Cambridge University Press, Cambridge Great Britain.

Wright, H. A. and A. W. Bailey. 1982. Fire ecology: United States and Southern Canada. John Wiley and Sons, New York.

Wright, H. A., S. C. Bunting, and L. F. Neuenschwander. 1976. Effect of fire on honey mesquite. Journal of range management **29**:467-471.

Chapter 2. Annotated information resources

2.1 Web fire resources

http://www.fire.org/
Fire software and publications developed by Systems for Environmental Management.

http://fireecology.okstate.edu/index.html
Basic fire ecology and fire effects, detailed analysis of heterogeneity on rangelands (systems for creating and effects of). Links to more information and contacts. Pdfs of published works available.

http://frames.nbii.gov/portal/server.pt?open=512&objID=213&mode=2&in_hi_userid=2&cached=true
Click on documents for research reports on fire effects, tools for fire software. Links for other fire related websites.

http://www.fs.fed.us/database/feis/index.html
(FEIS) Fire Effects Information System. Lots of information from invasives, plants, animals, to fire regimes. Publications can be ordered for free. Here is a list of some well written synthesis papers downloadable from FEIS:
RMRS-GTR-42-vol. 1. Wildland fire in ecosystems: effects of fire on fauna
RMRS-GTR-42-vol. 2. Wildland fire in ecosystems: effects of fire on flora
RMRS-GTR-42-vol. 4. Wildland fire in ecosystems: effects of fire on soils and water
RMRS-GTR-42-vol. 5. Wildland fire in ecosystems: effects of fire on air
RMRS-GTR-42-vol. 6. Wildland fire in ecosystems: fire and nonnative invasive plants

http://www.iawfonline.org/links.php
International association of wildland fire. Many links to fire related materials.

http://www.nps.gov/fire/fire/fir_ecology.cfm
National Park Service fire information including research, monitoring handbook and links to other fire related materials.

http://www.oklahomaprescribedfirecouncil.okstate.edu/Fire_Information.html
Links to related fact sheets from various sources.

http://www.talltimbers.org/
Fire ecology conference publications, research, and information

http://www.wfas.net/
Wildland fire assessment system includes weather information, drought maps, indices, ect.

2.2 Annotated bibliography of vital fire ecology research by category
 (*text included in companion to resource kit).

Catagories (Right click on category to navigate directly to it): fire, grassland ecology, heterogeneity, management, restoration, and miscellaneous

Fire   *Photo by Angela Smith*

Bond, W. J. and B. W. van Wilgen. 1996. Fire and Plants. Population and community biology series 14, Chapman and Hall, London. *Plant physiological, evolutionary, and community responses to fire.*

*Briggs, J. M., A. K. Knapp, and B. L. Brock. 2002. Expansion of woody plants in tallgrass prairie: a fifteen-year study of fire and fire-grazing interactions. American Midland Naturalist **147**:287-294. *Woody plants at Konza prairie have expanded in all treatments (fire intervals and grazing) except for annual burning without grazing.*

Collins, S. L. and Wallace, L. L. (editors). 1990. Fire in North American tallgrass prairies. University of Oklahoma Press, Norman Oklahoma. *Chapters in this book review grassland ecology work done at Konza Prairie, KS. It includes the effects of fire on a variety of tallgrass prairie components such as plants, communities, small mammals, and diversity. A worthwhile investment.*

Daubenmire, R. 1968. Ecology of fire in grasslands. Advances in Ecological Research 5:209-266. *A comprehensive view of fire in grasslands including soils and plants.*

*Earls, P. 2006. Prairie fire history of the tallgrass prairie National Preserve and the Flint Hills, Kansas. Unpublished manuscript submitted to the National Park Service, Omaha, Nebraska. *Review of fire in the Flint Hills through three different time periods. Provides references to historical accounts and information on fire origins, use, and effects.*

Engle, D. M., M. W. Palmer, J. S. Crockett, R. L. Mitchell, and R. Stevens. 2000. Influence of late season fire on early successional vegetation of an Oklahoma prairie. Journal of Vegetation Science 11:135-144. *Effects of summer fire on species composition and richness were inconclusive.*

*Frost, C. C. 1998. Presettlement fire frequency regimes of the United States: a first

approximation. Pages 70-81 *in* T. L. Pruden, and L. A. Brennan, editors. Fire in ecosystem management: shifting the paradigm from suppression to prescription. Tall Timbers Research Station, Tallahassee, FL. *Sets the stage for understanding fire frequency intervals by describing the effect of landscape fragmentation and seasonality. Ecological fire effects are influenced by abiotic and biotic factors. A fire frequency map is presented.*

Gibson, D. J., and L. C. Hulbert. 1987. Effects of fire, topography ,and year-to-year climatic variation on species composition in tallgrass prairie. Vegetatio **72**:175-185. *Species richness declines with time since burn. Topography and climate also regulate species so that species appear to have individual responses to fire.*

Gibson, D. J. 1988. Regeneration and fluctuation of tallgrass prairie vegetation in response to burning frequency. Bulletin of the Torrey Botanical Club **115**:1-12. *Landscape heterogeneity and secondarily burning explained community dynamics.*

*Guyette, R. P., Muzika, R. M. and D. C. Dey. 2002. Dynamics of an anthropogenic fire regime. Ecosystems **5**:472-486. *Discusses a human population dependent model of fire use to resistance to burning.*

*Guyette, R. P., D. C. Dey, M. C. Stambaugh, R. Muzika. 2006. Fire scars reveal variability and dynamics of eastern fire regimes. Pages 20-39 *in* M. B. Dickinson, editor. Fire in eastern oak forests: delivering science to land managers, proceedings of a conference, 2005 November 15-17; Columbus, OH. Gen. Tech. Rep. NRS-P-1. Newtown Square, PA: U.S. Department of Agriculture, Forest Service, Northern Research Station. *Describe a model to calculate fire return intervals based on precipitation, temperature, and human populations.*

Hartnett, D. C., K. R. Hickman, and L. E. Fischer Walter. 1996. Effects of bison grazing, fire, and topography on floristic diversity in tallgrass prairie. Journal of Range Management. **49**:413-420. *Species responded diversely to bison grazing and fire but species diversity and spatial heterogeneity increased.*

Stewart, O.C. 2002. Forgotten Fires: Native Americans and the Transient Wilderness. H. T. Lewis and M. K. Anderson, editors. University of Oklahoma Press, Norman. Pp 364.

Whelan, R. J. 1995. The ecology of fire. Cambridge University Press, Cambridge Great Britain. *Fire effects on plants, animals, and communities.*

Grassland ecology   *Photo by Sarah Douglas*

*Anderson, R. C. 2006. Evolution and origin of the Central Grassland of North America: climate, fire, and mammalian grazers. Journal of the Torrey Botanical Society **133**:626-647. *A classic paper on the evolution of grasslands in the Great Plains.*

*Axelrod, D. I. 1985. Rise of the grassland biome, Central North America. The Botanical Review **51**:163-201. *The evolutionary history of grasslands in North America is presented including the role of fire and large ungulates.*

Bragg, T. B. 1995. The physical environment of Great Plains grasslands. Pages 49-81 *in* A. Joern and K. H. Keeler, editors. The changing prairie. Oxford University Press, New York. *Describes factors contributing to grassland dynamics such as soil, topography, climate, the effects of fire on a variety of organisms and management considerations.*

*Briske, D. D., S.D. Fuhlendorf, and F. E. Smeins. 2003. Vegetation dynamics on rangelands: a critique of the current paradigms. Journal of Applied Ecology **40**:601-614. *Reviews succession theory (equilibrium and nonequalibrium) with respect to explaining grassland phenomena. Current paradigms acknowledge the role of environmental stochastisity.*

Knapp, A. K., J. M. Blair, J. M. Briggs, S. L. Collins, D. C. Hartnett, and L. C. Johnson. 1999. The keystone role of bison in North American tallgrass prairie. Bioscience **49**:39-50. *Emphasizes the important role bison once played in North American grasslands.*

*McClain, W. E. and S. L. Elzinga. 1994. The occurrence of prairie and forest fires in Illinois and other Midwestern states, 1679 to 1854. Erigenia **13**:79-90. *Includes historical accounts of Native American and early settler use of fire.*

Heterogeneity

Anderson, R. H., S. D. Fuhlendorf, and D. M. Engle. 2006. Soil nitrogen availability in tallgrass prairie under the fire-grazing interaction. Rangeland Ecology & Management **59**:625-631. *Soil nitrogen changes with movement of burn-grazed patches.*

Bakker, C., J. M. Blair, and A. K. Knapp. 2003. Does resource availability, resource heterogeneity or species turnover mediate changes in plant species richness in grazed grasslands? Oecologia **137**:385-391. *Argues that spatial heterogeneity of light and higher rates of species turnover were associated greater species richness in grazed areas.*

Collins, S. L. 1992. Fire frequency and community heterogeneity in tallgrass prairie vegetation. Ecology **73**:2001-2006. *Heterogeneity was lower in an annually burned prairie than unburned, or burned every four years. Within site heterogeneity was positively correlated to total richness and species diversity. Relationships differed at large scales.*

*Collins, S. L., and M. D. Smith. 2006. Scale-dependent interaction of fire and grazing on community heterogeneity in tallgrass prairie. Ecology **87**:2058-2067. *Corroborates Fuhlendorf and Engle's findings that the fire and grazing interaction changes the patterns of heterogeneity in rangeland.*

*Fuhlendorf, S. D. and D. M. Engle. 2001. Restoring heterogeneity on rangelands: ecosystem management based on evolutionary grazing patterns. Bioscience **51**:625-632. *Rangelands are traditionally managed for homogeneity which leads to loss of biodiversity. They argue that management techniques, such as patch burning, that aim to produce heterogeneous landscapes will better support biodiversity.*

*Fuhlendorf, S. D., W. C. Harrell, and D. M. Engle. 2006. Should heterogeneity be the basis for conservation? Grassland bird response to fire and grazing. Ecological Applications **16**:1706-1716. *Grassland bird species composition responds to heterogeneity created by burning and grazing.*

*Pickett, S. T. A., and M. L. Cadenasso. 1995. Landscape ecology: spatial heterogeneity in ecological systems. Science **269**:331-334. *Describes the role of heterogeneity in landscape ecology.*

Rotenberry, J. T. and J. A. Wiens. 1990. Habitat structure, patchiness, and avian communities in North American steppe vegetation: a multivariate analysis. Ecology **61**:1228-1250.

*Tews, J., U. Brose, V. Grimm, K. Tielbörger, M. C. Wichmann, M. Schwager, and F. Jeltsch. 2004. Animal species diversity driven by habitat heterogeneity/diversity: the importance of keystone structures. Journal of Biogeography **31**:79-92. *Meta analysis that found many studies have positive correlation between heterogeneity and species richness but the effect varies by spatial scale and organism.*

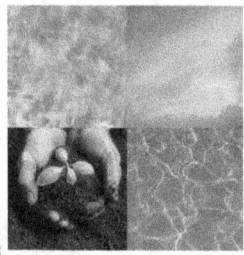

Management

*Evans, J. E. 1983. Literature review of management practices for smooth sumac (*Rhus glabra*), poison ivy (*Rhus radicans*) and other sumac species. Natural Areas Journal **3**:16-26. *Outline of management practices for some problematic woody species in grasslands.*

*Davies, K. W., and R. L. Sheley. 2007. A conceptual framework for preventing the spatial dispersal of invasive plants. Weed Science **55**:178-184. *Describes a model and example for preventing dispersal of invasive plants.*

Gibson, D. J., T. R. Seastedt, and J. M. Briggs. 1993. Management practices in tallgrass prairie: large- and small-scale experimental effects on species composition. Journal of Applied Ecology **30**:247-255. *At the largest scale, soil type was the driver of species composition. At smaller scales burning, fertilizer, and mowing differed in effects on species.*

Hobbs, R. J., and L. F. Huenneke. 1992. Disturbance, diversity, and invasion: implications for conservation. Conservation biology **6**:324-337. *Disturbances outside the historical regime can contribute to invasive species proliferation. Historical patterns often are not applicable under current conditions so critical decisions must be made to control or accept species.*

*Masters, R. E., and R. L. Sheley. 2001. Principles and practices for managing rangeland invasive plants. Journal of Range Management. **54**:502-517. *Describes types of invasive plant management, uses and action of herbicides, and strategies.*

*Richburg, J. A., A. C. Dibble, and W. A. Patterson, III. 2001. Woody invasive species and their role in altering fire regimes of the Northeast and Mid-Atlantic states. Pages 104–111 *in* K. E. M. Galley and T. P. Wilson, editors. Proceedings of the Invasive Species Workshop: the Role of Fire in the Control and Spread of Invasive Species. Fire Conference 2000. The First National Congress on Fire Ecology, Prevention, and Management. Miscellaneous Publication No. 11, Tall Timbers Research Station, Tallahassee, FL. *Reviews several species biology and control measures. The authors emphasize appropriate timing of treatments.*

Tunnell, S. J., J. Stubbendieck, and S. Palazzolo. 2006. Forb response to herbicides in a degraded tallgrass prairie. Natural Areas Journal **26**:72-77. *Study of forb response to management practices for sumac in grasslands.*

*Tunnell, S. J., J. Stubbendieck, S. Palazzolo, and R. A. Masters. 2006. Reducing smooth sumac dominance in native tallgrass prairie. Great Plains Research **16**:45-49. *Study of management practices for sumac in grasslands.*

Restoration   *Photo by Angela Smith*

Palmer, M. A., R. F. Ambrose, and N. L. Poff. 1997. Ecological theory and community
    restoration ecology. Restoration Ecology **5**:291-300. *Outlines goals for an ecological
    approach to restoration.*

Society for Ecological Restoration International Science & Policy Working Group. The SER
    International Primer on Ecological Restoration. 2004. 1-13. www.ser.org & Tuscon:
    Society for Ecological Restoration International. *A good outline for guiding restoration
    efforts. Provides steps and outlines ecological reasons for conducting restorations.*

Miscellaneous   *Photo by Sarah Douglas*

*Maestas, J. D., R. L. Knight, and W. C. Gilgert. 2003. Biodiversity across a rural land use-
    gradient. Conservation biology **17**:1425-1434. *Habitat fragmentation caused by ranches
    being subdivided and developed into ranchettes lead to change in avian species
    composition and diversity.*

*Samson, F., and F. Knopf. 1994. Prairie conservation in North America. Bioscience **44**:418-
    414. *Builds a case for emphasis on grassland conservation.*

Tilman, D., P. B. Reich, J. Knops, D. Wedin, T. Mielke, and C. Lehman. 2001. Diversity and
    productivity in a long-term grassland experiment. Science **294**:843-845. *Demonstrated in
    small cultivated plots that productivity and carbon storage were greater in more diverse
    assemblages.*

Chapter 3. Who do I call for help?

Because of the extensive geographic variation within the Heartland Network, it would be difficult to provide specific recommendations for each element you are considering treating with fire within a single document. Please contact Heartland staff or NPS fire specialists with specific questions and we will assist you with developing solutions.

Fire ecology contacts: http://www.nps.gov/fire/fire/fir_eco_contacts.cfm

Heartland Network home page: http://science.nature.nps.gov/im/units/htln/index.cfm

Midwest Region Fire Management Program, Regional Fire Ecologist (402) 661-1770

The Department of the Interior protects and manages the nation's natural resources and cultural heritage; provides scientific and other information about those resources; and honors its special responsibilities to American Indians, Alaska Natives, and affiliated Island Communities.

NPS D-72, February 2008

Natural Resource Program Center
1201 Oakridge Drive, Suite 150
Fort Collins, CO 80525

www.nature.nps.gov